Vintage Style *for* Kids

First published in 2010 by Jacqui Small,
7 Greenland Street, London NW1 0ND

Publisher Jacqui Small
Editorial Manager Kerenza Swift
Commissioning Editor Zia Mattocks
Art Director Barbara Zuñiga
Illustrator Kate Simunek
Stylist Sara Burke
Production Peter Colley

ISBN 978 1 906417 44 4
A catalogue record for this book is available
from the British Library.
2012 2011 2010

10 9 8 7 6 5 4 3 2 1

Printed and bound in China

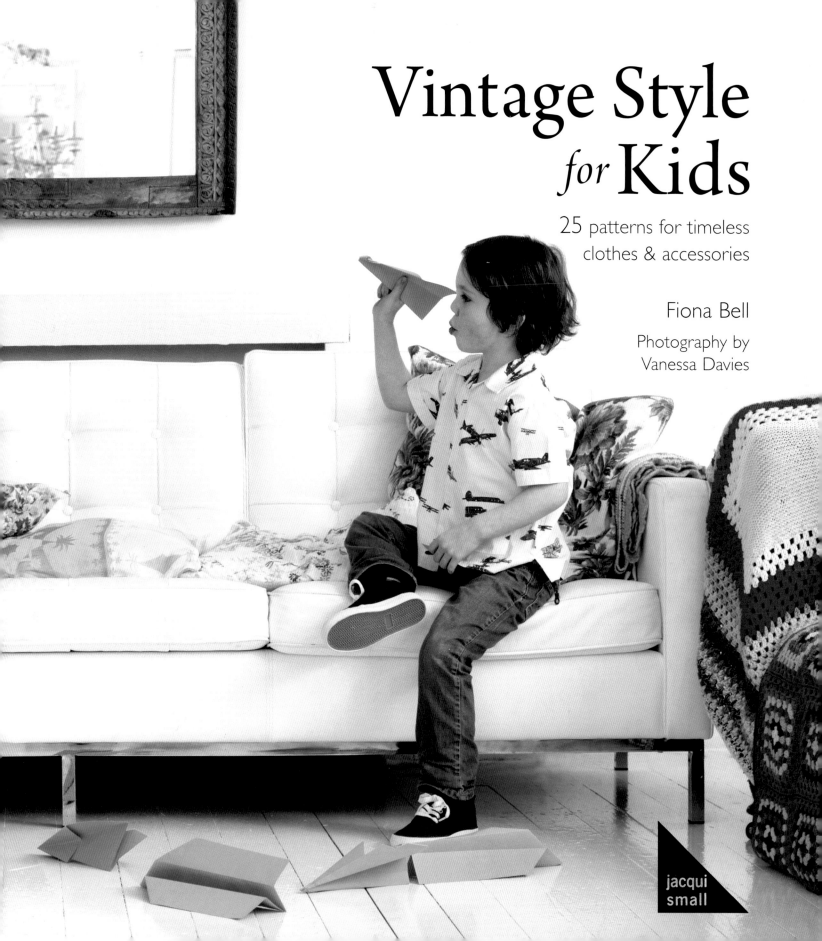

Vintage Style
for Kids

25 patterns for timeless
clothes & accessories

Fiona Bell

Photography by
Vanessa Davies

jacqui
small

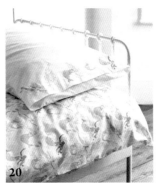

Contents

Introduction: Vintage Style   6

Babies   14

1 Baby's Dress & Sun Hat   16
2 Playsuit   22
3 Baby's Bubble   28
4 Vintage Quilt   32

Playtime   36

5 Button-Through Dress   38
6 Dirndl Skirt   42
7 Dungarees   46
8 Madras-Check Shorts   50
9 Classic Shirt   54
10 Cover-All Apron   60
11 Boy's Short-Sleeved Shirt   64
12 Notice Board   70
13 Beanbag Frog   72

Parties   74

14 Full-Circle Dress   76
15 Silk-Chiffon & Lace Dress   82
16 Tulip-Shaped Dress   88
17 Handkerchief-Sleeve Dress   94
18 1950s Pin-Tuck Dress   100
19 Boy's Pin-Tuck Shirt   108

Bedtime   114

20 Duvet Set   116
21 Classic Boy's Pyjamas   120
22 Girl's Summer Pyjamas   126
23 Laundry/Toy Bag   132
24 Tooth Fairy Pillow   136

Templates   140
Sewing Guidelines & Tips   141
Making the Paper Patterns   142
Size Guide   142
Address Book   143
Acknowledgements   144

Introduction: Vintage Style

The beauty of vintage clothes is that they evoke the nostalgia that goes with their heritage. Dressing children in vintage-inspired clothes makes them look like children rather than mini adults, which is so often the vibe of many of the labels available today. Vintage prints, trims and silhouettes give clothes a kind of timeless elegance – in fact, the term 'vintage' has become enshrined in the fashion world's terminology, referring to a classic item of clothing.

The inspiration behind my own label, Their Nibs, was my absolute love of vintage clothing and, in particular, prints, which have always been a passion of mine and are the mainstay of my collections. I find inspiration for new prints from so many different sources – for example, old greetings cards, vintage pottery and even vintage playing cards, which often have amazing designs on the reverse. One print featured in this book, Spanish Dancing Girls (see page 100), was inspired by an old set of cards bought in Camden Market, north London. Another (used for the Button-Through Dress on page 38) came from a fabulous old tea set bought from a vintage fair in Chelsea. It is such a pleasure attending these fairs, along with my

mainstay of inspiration, the wonderful Portobello Road Market in Notting Hill. Markets are a hive of colour and design from so many aspects, and London, along with New York and Paris, has an abundance of them.

The shapes of vintage clothes are an inspiration in themselves; they are so inventive and make children look like they are supposed to look for those first precious years of their lives: like children. Vintage-inspired and genuine vintage clothing for kids does not have to be 'prissy' and can look as relevant when styled in the right way as the most high-fashion clothing items. Many of the classic vintage shapes for boys evoke those early years so effortlessly – dressing your toddler in soft cord dungarees and vintage printed shirts is so much more original than run-of-the-mill branded T-shirts and jeans. Old dressmaking patterns are a great source of inspiration for new shapes – the classic Girl's Summer Pyjamas (see page 126) were based on an old American sewing pattern found on eBay.

There are so many silhouettes that I have produced over the years and I have many favourite designs. Often a shape in my collection can run for many seasons, even years, and the two that have proved to have longevity and always seem to look new and fresh when translated into a different print are the Baby's Bubble and the Full-Circle Dress (see pages 28 and 76). The Baby's Bubble romper is a shape that lends itself so well to vintage fabrics and has that 'wow' factor for a newborn's first outfit, while the Full-Circle Dress is perennially popular with little girls. Changing the prints and trims used on garments is the perfect way to update them, without always changing the silhouettes.

The impetus for starting my business in 2002 was twofold. Firstly, having worked in the fashion industry for nearly 20 years and understanding what made a brand, I could see a gap in the market for a vintage-inspired, vibrant and inventive alternative to the brands offered in the childrenswear market. Secondly, one of my biggest inspirations was 'his Nibs', my very lively son Finn Luca Faed, who has been with me all the way along this incredible journey creating Their Nibs, from a crazy 2-year-old to a now equally crazy 9-year-old. He has always had, and continues to have, the most adventurous and innovative dress sense – being able to mix vintage pieces with skateboarding clothing: pure genius.

Left I find moodboards are a great way of pulling ideas together for new collections. They help me channel an eclectic mix of inspirations – such as old lace, buttons, and new prints ideas – into a cohesive collection.

Opposite Every woman remembers her favourite childhood party dress, and pretty dresses in prints and plains give a lovely vintage feel for a special occasion. Little girls look like little girls and mothers can treasure those special memories.

Left Vintage dressmaking patterns are a great source of inspiration for shapes and details to incorporate in new designs.

Opposite top left Broderie anglaise lace is used a lot in children's vintage clothing and works well when combined with prints, such as this orange-and-white spotted yoke. The lace edge on the placket of the dress completes the look, along with the interesting buttons with contrast edges.

Opposite top right 'Handkerchief' sleeves are such a pretty, feminine styling detail on a dress, and a typical feature of vintage garments from the 1970s. They fan out when worn, making them great fun, too.

Vintage Silhouettes

The spectrum of vintage shapes, of everything from dresses to boys' shirts, means there is an almost endless source of blank canvases for creative experimentation with decorative details in the form of buttons, lace and trims.

A distinctive feature of dress shapes that epitomize the vintage look is a full skirt, often tiered, which provides a magical way for little girls to enjoy the 'twirling' effect of the dress when worn. A tiered frill on the hem of a skirt or dress is a classic detail, and can be finished with picot-edge lace on the base of the hem. Yokes on dresses, in either a matching or contrasting fabric, as shown above and on the Button-Through Dress (see page 38), are another characteristic design element.

Sleeve shapes offer other possibilities for giving a garment a vintage feel. A 'handkerchief' sleeve, such as the one on the dress above (see page 94), is a lovely floaty sleeve that works well in a number of different fabrics, from cotton voile to baby cord. A lamp-shade sleeve is also a classic – the sleeve is tight at the elbow and then gathers out to form a 'lamp-shade' shape, often with a lace trim at the elbow point or sleeve end. 'Angel' sleeves are another delightful detail; the Button-Through Dress and Baby's Dress (see page 16) have typical 'angel' sleeves.

Archetypal silhouettes for boys include single-breasted formal jackets, an exaggerated collar point on shirts, or collar reveres on 1950s box-shaped shirts (see pages 54 and 64).

Right and opposite, bottom left
The smocking stitch used on this dress is quite exquisite. Hand-smocking is an art form in itself. Here it not only makes a great decorative feature on the garment, but it is also an intrinsic styling element that helps to define the dress's shape.

Opposite, top left This classic baby's all-in-one features smocking-stitch detail on the yoke combined with a lovely 'Peter Pan' collar. The collar itself has tiny hand-sewn blanket stitching around the edge, completing the garment's attention to detail.

Opposite, top right Rickrack lace is a traditional vintage trim that is often used on baby's or girl's dresses, but can also be found on smock blouses or even outerwear, such as summer coats. On this baby's dress, the trim is delicate and in keeping with the design, but provides the added detail that gives the garment a point of difference.

Opposite, bottom right Picot lace edging, such as the one found on this floral baby's dress, is another very typical decorative trim found on vintage garments. Because it can be used as an edging trim, it is often found on knitted cardigans as well as woven garments.

Vintage Details

It's the little details that keep children's vintage style looking so timeless and fresh. Trims and clever stitching are key – smocking, rickrack, pleating and lace make an outfit unique and are a big part of the childish quirkiness that we love. Adding one or more of these touches to any design is an easy way to make something run-of-the-mill special, and to make kids' clothes look just as gorgeous, inspirational and exciting to them as they do to us.

Treasuring Your Finds

When you own vintage garments, you can be sure that these gorgeous pieces have been cherished and loved by a previous owner. They, like you, did not subscribe to a throwaway society. In order to keep these treasures in pristine condition, the following tips may be useful.

Storing

Before storing, give vintage clothes a good airing on the washing line, but be sure to keep them out of the sun, as sunlight can fade colours and damage the fibres in old fabrics.

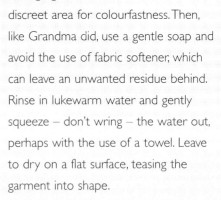

- Fragile items are best stored flat because of the risk of stretching. A useful trick is to use acid-free tissue paper or acid-free boxes, as acids can yellow or break down fibres. Never store vintage garments in plastic, because it can create a humid atmosphere that may lead to mildew setting in.
- Garments can be rolled to prevent stressed fibres at creases.
- Linen or cotton sachets filled with dried lavender, rosemary and mint will deter moths – and they smell far nicer than moth balls.
- If you do use a hanger, make sure it is a softly padded one, and that the garment sits comfortably on it. The shoulder ends of hangers can do untold damage to fibres and could make the piece misshapen.

Laundering

Take great care here. Fabrics need to be identified and treated by either professional dry cleaners or a wise owner.

- Silk, chiffon and velvet need to be professionally cleaned. Always check with your dry cleaner that the machinery and chemicals they use are going to be compatible with the fabric, as high temperatures could weaken fragile material and melt buttons.
- When laundering a vintage garment at home, test a small, discreet area for colourfastness. Then, like Grandma did, use a gentle soap and avoid the use of fabric softener, which can leave an unwanted residue behind. Rinse in lukewarm water and gently squeeze – don't wring – the water out, perhaps with the use of a towel. Leave to dry on a flat surface, teasing the garment into shape.
- When ironing a vintage garment, it is a good idea to iron on the wrong side to prevent iron marks. Velvet should not be ironed but hung up in a steamy bathroom, or you can use steam from a steam iron. When it is cool, gently brush down the nap.

Top Tip Having taken all this care with your treasure, why not give it pride of place and display it as a feature for a while? Vintage clothes can add a really special touch to a child's room. Remember, though, they do not like sunlight or damp conditions.

Wearing Vintage

The most satisfying thing about the look of a vintage outfit is its wide appeal for everyone – from a proud grandma to the trendiest mum. Grandma may style a vintage dress in a more traditional way, with a ballet-wrap cardigan and ballet-style pumps, but the same dress could be worn with a pair of battered canvas shoes and a long-sleeved T-shirt underneath – as styled by Mum.

Vintage is such a versatile area of kids' fashion that current items, such as leggings, sheepskin boots and ubiquitous jeans, can all be teamed to great effect with vintage pieces. A boy's formal vintage jacket looks amazing when dressed down with skinny jeans and a vintage T-shirt, for example.

Customizing vintage clothes is another way of achieving an individual look and is lots of fun to do with kids. My son loves to add interesting buttons to jackets and collects old woven badges from markets to use, too. There is something truly lovely about seeing an old button that belonged to your grandma reused in a decorative way on a piece of your child's clothing.

Opposite Self-fabric bows are a lovely way to add a trim on a dress that doesn't need lace to give that attention to detail. The print on this dress with the classic 'Peter Pan' collar is so delicate that the two self-fabric bows are enough to complete the look and let the print speak for itself.

Above right Gorgeous pieces of lace, trims and vintage buttons give a wonderful point of difference to children's clothes.

Right Vintage shapes can be brought bang up to date when teamed with accessories such as leggings and funky shoes.

Babies

The arrival of a new baby is a perfect time to harness the creativity that new life brings. These vintage-inspired patterns will help you to create practical pieces that will become, in time, precious handmade heirlooms to pass down to the next generation. Inspired by yesteryear, to last a lifetime.

Baby's Dress & Sun Hat

With its classic-vintage angel sleeves, this is a really pretty dress shape for a baby. The frilled pockets on the front of the skirt, which could be trimmed with fine lace with a pique edge for additional decoration, are a lovely detail. For a summer version of the dress, a good grade cotton poplin or cotton voile in a charming print are great choices. Alternatively, use plain cotton poplin and decorate the front of the dress with appliqué or embroidery. The hat can be made in a matching or contrasting print. For winter, a fine grade (such as 19 wale) baby cord would work well; team it with woolly tights and a cosy bolero cardigan.

Materials

Paper for pattern
2.2m (2½yd) printed cotton
    voile for outer
1.65m (2yd) plain cotton voile
    for lining
3 buttons, 1cm (⅜in) diameter
Basting thread
Matching sewing thread
Sewing machine and sewing kit
Iron and ironing board

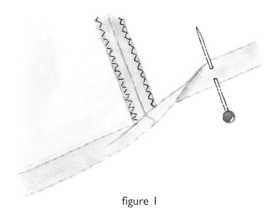

figure 1

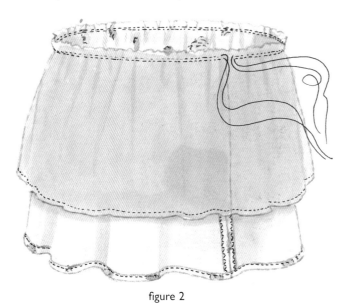

figure 2

STEP 1
Starting the skirt

With right sides together, pin, baste and machine stitch the front and back of the skirt along the side seams; finish the raw edges and press the seams.

Fold the hem 5mm (¼in) to the wrong side and press, then fold over and press another 5mm (¼in) and machine stitch the hem. Repeat for the shorter-length lining (see *figure 1*).

STEP 2
Building the gathers

With wrong sides together, and matching the side seams, pin the lining to the skirt around the waistline. Leaving long threads at both ends, sew a row of gathering stitching around the top of the skirt, 5mm (¼in) in from the edge. Sew a second row 3mm (⅛in) below the first. Hold one end of both threads on the right side of the fabric and gather up the material until the top of the skirt is the same width as the bodice (excluding the seam allowance). Evenly distribute the gathers around the skirt (see *figure 2*).

STEP 3

Making the bodice

With right sides together, sew the front and back bodices together at the shoulders and side seams; press the seams open. Repeat for the lining. Pin the lining and bodice with wrong sides together and sew around the neckline, 5mm (¼in) from the edge.

With the lining and outer fabric together, fold and press the raw edges of the back opening 5mm (¼in) to the wrong side. Then fold the button plackets to the wrong side along the fold lines, and press. Sew along the hemmed edge of the button plackets, from the neckline to the bottom of the bodice. Overlap the left placket over the right and tack in place at the bottom of the bodice (see *figure 3*).

Adjusting the gathers on the skirt as necessary, pin and baste the bodice to the skirt with right sides together, then machine stitch 5mm (¼in) from the edge. Overlock the raw edges.

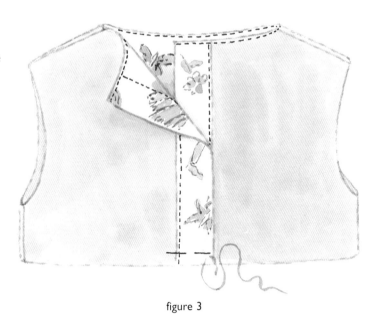

figure 3

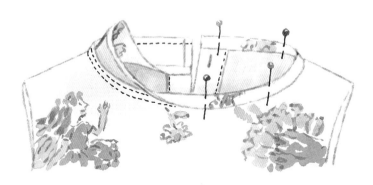

figure 4

STEP 4

Finishing the neckline

Press the short ends of the trim (which is cut on the bias) 5mm (¼in) to the wrong side; press one long edge 5mm (¼in) to the wrong side. With the right side of the trim to the lining of the dress, align the raw edge of the trim with the inside of the neckline. Make sure the ends of the trim align with the edge of the button plackets, then sew 5mm (¼in) from the edge. Flip the folded edge to the right side of the dress and topstitch around the neckline close to the folded edge (see *figure 4*).

Make three vertical buttonholes on the top button placket, positioning the first 5mm (¼in) below the bottom of the trim and in the centre of the placket. Sew three corresponding buttons on the bottom button placket.

STEP 5

Making the sleeves

Apply decorative stay stitching to the outer edge of the sleeves, or hem them.

Gather the cap of the sleeves in the same way as you gathered the top of the skirt (see *step 2*).

With right sides together, fit a sleeve into each armhole, aligning the centre of the gathered edge with the shoulder seam. Sew 5mm (¼in) from the edge, then overlock the raw edges (see *figure 5*).

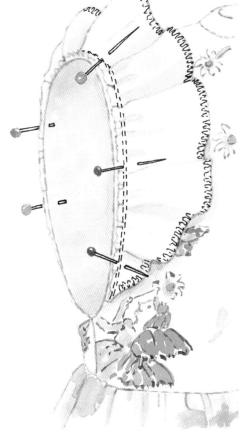

figure 5

STEP 6

Finishing the armholes

Press the short ends of the seam binding (which is cut on the bias) 5mm (¼in) to the wrong side. Press the top and bottom edges of the seam binding 5mm (¼in) to the wrong side. Fold and press the seam allowance at the bottom of the armhole to the wrong side of the dress. Pin and then baste the binding to the bottom of the armhole, just covering the ends of the sleeve, and then topstitch all around the edge (see *figure 6*).

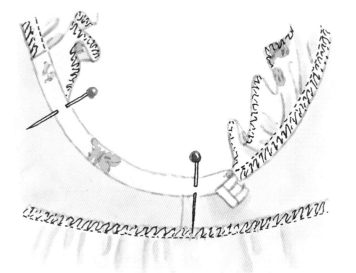

figure 6

STEP 7

Adding the pockets

Apply decorative stay stitching to the bottom of the pocket frills. Gather the top of the frills to match the width of the pockets. With the wrong side of the frill to the right side of the pocket, pin and baste together along the top edge.

Press the bottom edge of the pocket trims 5mm (¼in) to the wrong side. With the right side of the trim to the wrong side of the pocket, line up the raw edge of the trim with the top inside edge of the pocket, and sew 5mm (¼in) from the edge. Flip the folded edge of the trim to the outside of the pocket and topstitch (see *figure 7*).

Press the sides and bottom of the pockets 5mm (¼in) to the wrong side. Sew a few gathering stitches along the centre bottom of the pockets and gather the fabric slightly to give the pockets fullness.

Topstitch the two pockets onto the front of the skirt, making sure they are equal distances from the side seams and waistline.

figure 7

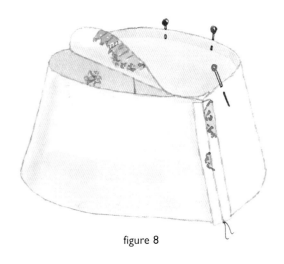

figure 8

STEP 8

Making up the cap of the sun hat

With right sides together, pin and baste the two pieces of the cap together along the side seams to form a cylinder. Machine stitch with 5mm (¼in) seams, and press the seams open.

With right sides together, fit the circular piece for the crown into the top of the cylinder, aligning the raw edges (see *figure 8*). Sew with a 5mm (¼in) seam allowance. Repeat for the lining.

Fold and press the bottom edge of the cap and lining 5mm (¼in) to the wrong side.

STEP 9

Making the brim

Sew the ends of the brim together with a French seam. Do this by pinning and basting the ends of the strip with wrong sides together; machine stitch close to the raw edge. Turn the brim inside out and fold the fabric right sides together along the line of stitching. Pin, baste and machine stitch 5mm (¼in) from the sewn edge to enclose the raw edges. Press the seam to one side and topstitch along the edge.

Fold and press the bottom edge of the brim 5mm (¼in) to the wrong side. Fold over and press another 5mm (¼in), and sew the hem in place (see *figure 9*).

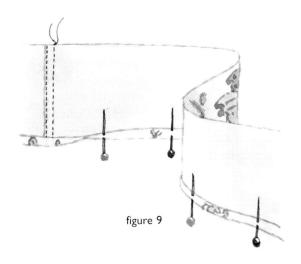

figure 9

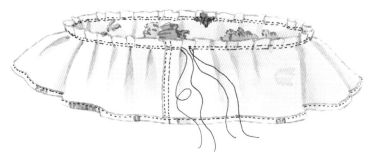

figure 10

STEP 10

Gathering the brim

Leaving long threads at both ends, sew a row of gathering stitching around the top of the brim, 5mm (¼in) in from the raw edge. Sew a second row 3mm (⅛in) below the first. Holding one end of the threads tightly, gently gather up the material until the gathered edge of the brim is the same width as the bottom of the cap, making sure the gathers are evenly distributed (see *figure 10*).

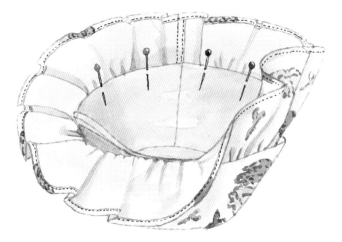

figure 11

STEP 11

Sewing the hat together

Put the lining into the crown with wrong sides together. Push the seam allowance of the gathered edge of the brim between the folded edges of the lining and the outer fabric of the cap, making sure the right side of the brim is facing out. Pin and baste in place, then topstitch along the folded edge (see *figure 11*).

Playsuit

The inspiration for this charming and practical baby's playsuit came from a garment I found at a vintage fair in Paris a few years ago. The attention to detail shown by the little bows on the pockets is indicative of how the French go that little bit further with styling touches.

For the colder months, the playsuit lends itself well to soft cord or chambray fabrics, to be worn with a long-sleeve jersey T-shirt. It works equally well in pretty poplin prints or even cotton voiles for the warmer weather.

Materials

Paper for pattern
1.5m (1¾yd) printed baby cord
   for outer and lining
12 buttons, 1cm (⅜in) diameter
Basting thread
Matching sewing thread
Sewing machine and sewing kit
Iron and ironing board

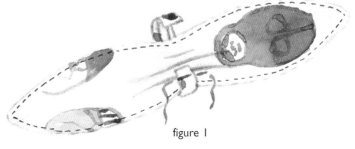

figure 1

STEP 1
Making the bows

Pin and then baste a front and back bow piece with right sides together. Machine stitch around the edge of the bow, leaving a 2.5cm (1in) gap in the bottom centre. Turn the bow right side out through the hole, fold the seam allowance inside, and topstitch all the way around the edge.

Fold both long sides of the 'bow fastener' to the centre, with wrong sides together, and tack them down. Tack one end of the strip centrally to the back top of the bow; pinch the bow together, and tack the other end of the strip centrally to the back bottom of the bow (see *figure 1*).

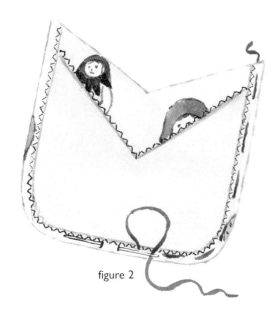

figure 2

STEP 2
Making the pockets

Sew zigzag stitch around the edges of the pocket and lining pieces. Then, with right sides together, sew the top of the pocket lining to the top of the pocket. Flip the lining to the inside and press. Fold the edges of the pocket 5mm (¼in) to the wrong side and press; pin and baste (see *figure 2*).

Topstitch the bows horizontally onto the top centre of the pockets, machine stitching vertically down both edges of the bow fasteners.

Pin and baste the pockets in position on the front leg pieces of the playsuit, then topstitch along the sides and bottom to secure.

STEP 3
Starting the bottoms

With right sides together, sew the bottoms together at the centre front seam and the side seams.

On the right-hand back piece, fold the button placket to the wrong side on the straight grain, and press. Clip into the left back piece at the bottom of the button placket. Fold the bottom edge 5mm (¼in) to the wrong side, and press. Then fold the left button placket to the wrong side, and pin and baste, ensuring the seam allowance at the bottom is enclosed within the fold.

Sew the centre back seam together, beginning below the button placket (see *figure 3*). Press all the seams open and finish the raw edges with zigzag stitch.

figure 3

STEP 4
Gathering the bottoms

Starting next to the button placket and leaving long threads at both ends, sew a row of gathering stitching 5mm (¼in) in from the edge across the top of the bottoms. Sew a second row 3mm (⅛in) below the first one (see *figure 4*).

Hold one end of the threads tightly and gently gather up the material until the bottoms are roughly the same width as the bottom of the front bodice piece. Distribute the gathers evenly all the way around.

figure 4

figure 5

STEP 5

The bottom button extensions

Fold and press the long edges of both button extensions 5mm (¼in) to the wrong side, then press them in half lengthways. Sew one raw edge of the button extension to the edge of the inside leg, with the right side of the extension to the wrong side of the playsuit. Flip the folded edge of the button extension to the right side, enclosing the raw edges within the fold of the extension, and pin and baste in place (see figure 5). Topstitch to secure, then topstitch along the outer edge of the button extension. Repeat for the other button extension on the other side of the playsuit bottoms.

This little piggy went to market.
This little piggy stayed at home.
This little piggy had roast beef,
This little piggy
    had none.
And this little piggy cried
    'Wee! Wee! Wee!'
    all the way home.

STEP 6

Finishing the legs

Leaving long threads at both ends, sew a row of gathering stitching 5mm (¼in) in from the edge along the bottom of each leg. Sew a second row 3mm (⅛in) below the first. Hold one end of the threads tightly and gather up the material until it is the width of the cuff piece, minus the seam allowance. Distribute the gathers evenly all the way around.

Fold and press the edges of the cuffs 5mm (¼in) to the wrong side. Press the cuffs in half lengthways. Align the right side of one raw edge of the cuff with the wrong side of the bottom of the leg and sew with a 5mm (¼in) seam allowance. Flip the folded side of the cuff to the right side, making sure the seam allowance at the ends is folded to the inside, and topstitch around the cuff. Repeat for the other leg.

Make seven horizontal buttonholes along the inside-leg extension on the front of the playsuit, positioning the first in the middle of the extension beneath the centre front seam. Space the other three evenly down both legs, with the last one in the middle of the cuffs, 5mm (¼in) from the edge. Sew corresponding buttons on the back button extension (see figure 6).

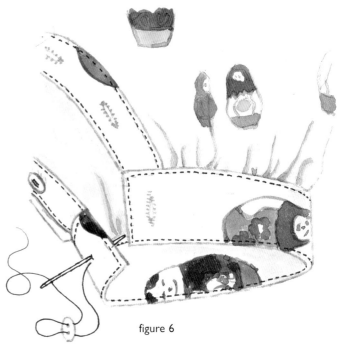

figure 6

STEP 7

Making the bodice

With right sides together, sew the front and back bodice pieces together at the shoulder and side seams. Press the seams open. Repeat for the lining.

With right sides facing, fit the lining and bodice together, and pin and then sew around the neckline and along the centre backs (see figure 7).

Turn the bodice right side out and press. Tuck the seam allowance of the armholes to the inside, and press. Align the folded edges of the lining and outer bodice around the armholes and baste together. Topstitch around the armholes, sewing just along the edge.

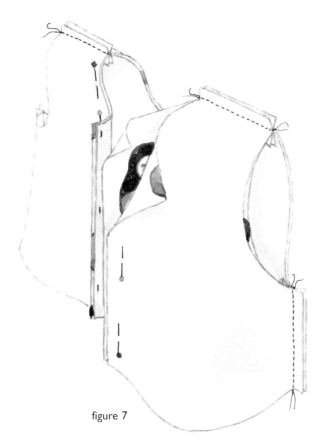

figure 7

figure 8

Monday's child is fair of face,
Tuesday's child is full of grace,
Wednesday's child is full of woe,
Thursday's child has far to go,
Friday's child is loving and giving,
Saturday's child works hard for a living,
But the child who is born on the Sabbath Day
Is bonny and blithe and good and gay.

STEP 8

Sewing the bodice and bottoms together

Sew zigzag stitching around the raw edges of the button plackets on the back of the playsuit bottoms.

With right sides together, line up the bottom edge of the bodice and lining with the top edge of the bottoms, starting at one button placket and making sure the edge of the bodice will be tucked neatly into the fold of the button placket when it is folded back. Sew the bodice and bottoms together, then overlock the seam.

Fold the button plackets to the wrong side of the playsuit. Make sure the seam allowance at the top of each placket is folded in, and topstitch the top of each placket along the seam that joins the bodice to the bottoms. Topstitch the bottom of the button plackets together where they overlap.

Sewing close to the edge, topstitch up one button placket, around the neckline and down the other button placket.

Make five vertical buttonholes on the left back opening, positioning them 1cm (½in) from the edge and spacing them evenly. Sew five corresponding buttons on the right back opening (see figure 8).

Baby's Bubble

The original garment on which this design is based came from a vintage clothing fair at Chelsea Town Hall in London. We adapted it slightly and named it the Bubble, a name that has stuck to this day. A best-seller in Their Nibs for the past few years, this is a gorgeous piece for newborns and toddlers. Because of its construction with the built-in pants under the frills, it is also highly practical.

When choosing a fabric, bear in mind the size of the pattern, as a larger-scale print will be lost, whereas a more delicate print, on cotton poplin for example, lends itself perfectly to this pretty, classic baby's garment.

Materials

Paper for pattern
1.75m (2yd) printed cotton
    fabric for outer and lining
Approximately 85cm (33½in)
    elastic, 5mm (¼in) wide
3 buttons, 1cm (⅜in) diameter
Basting thread
Matching sewing thread
Sewing machine and sewing kit
Iron and ironing board
Safety pin

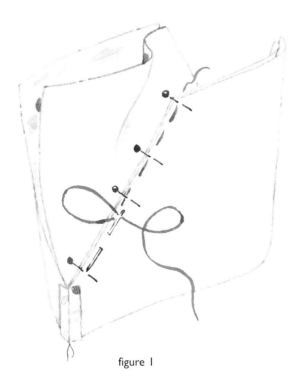

figure 1

STEP 1

Beginning the bodice

With right sides together, sew the side seams of the bodice together. Repeat for the lining. Press the seams open on both pieces.

With right sides together, pin and then baste the lining into the bodice around the armholes (see figure 1). Turn the bodice right side out, so the lining is on the inside, and press. Topstitch two rows around the armholes, one along the edge and the other 5mm (¼in) in.

Fold the bottom edges of the lining and the bodice 5mm (¼in) to the wrong side, and press.

STEP 2

Attaching the neck ruffles

For the double-layered ruffle at the neckline, take the wider strips first and, with right sides together, sew the side seams together to form a circle, and finish the raw edges. Fold the bottom edge 5mm (¼in) to the wrong side, and press, then fold over and press another 5mm (¼in) and sew along the edge of the hem. Repeat for the narrower strips.

Lay the right side of the bodice to the wrong side of the wider circle, and the right side of the narrower circle to the right side of the lining; align the raw edges, and pin and then sew along the neckline (see figure 2).

Flip the narrower strip to the right side, and topstitch along the seam allowance. Topstitch another row below the first, leaving a gap between the rows of stitching wide enough to fit the 5mm- (¼in-) wide elastic and leaving 2.5cm (1in) open at the centre back.

Cut a piece of elastic approximately half the circumference of the neckline. With a safety pin on one end to help push it through, thread the elastic through the channel and sew the ends together. Continue the two rows of topstitching to close the gap in the centre back.

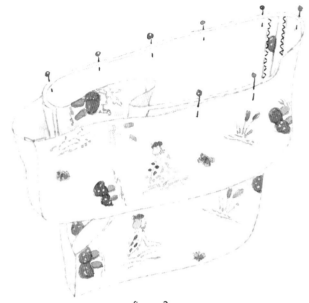

figure 2

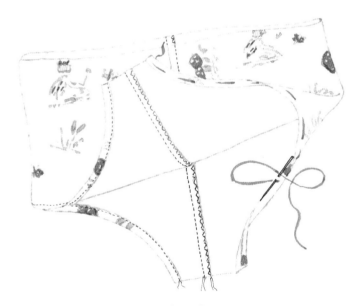

figure 3

STEP 3

Making up the pants

With right sides together, sew the left and right pieces of the pants together and finish the raw edges. Turn the pants right side out and topstitch along the fold of the seam.

Fold and press 5mm (¼in) to the wrong side around the leg holes. Fold the edges over again, creating a channel wide enough to fit the elastic through, and sew (see figure 3).

Cut two pieces of elastic approximately 20cm (8in) long. Using a safety pin, thread the elastic through the channels and tack it down at both ends.

STEP 4

Adding the buttons

Fold and press the four edges of both button extensions 5mm (¼in) to the wrong side, then press the extensions in half lengthways. Pin one button extension to the front of the pants and the other to the back, encasing the raw edges of the pants within the fold of the button extensions (see *figure 4*). Topstitch along all four sides of the button extensions, sewing close to the edge.

Make three horizontal buttonholes in the extension on the front of the pants, spacing them evenly. Sew three corresponding buttons in position on the right side of the back button extension.

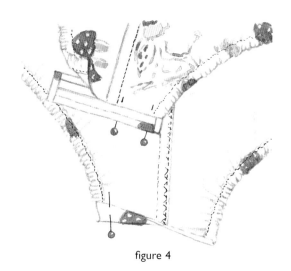

figure 4

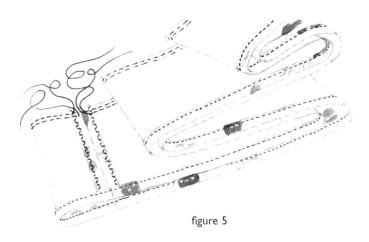

figure 5

STEP 5

Making the two 'skirt' frills

Sew up the side seams of the skirt frills in the same way as the neck ruffles and hem the bottom edges of both (see *first paragraph of step 2*).

Sew two rows of gathering stitching along the top edge of each frill, leaving long threads at both ends: sew the first row 5mm (¼in) in from the edge and the second row 3mm (¼in) below the first (see *figure 5*).

Holding the top threads on the narrower frill tightly, gather up the fabric until the gathered edge is the same width as the top of the pants. Ease the fabric gently to distribute the gathers evenly around the frill.

STEP 6

Sewing up the Baby's Bubble

With right sides together, sew up the side seams of the waistband, and finish the raw edges. Pin and baste the narrower frill to the top of the pants, aligning the wrong side of the gathered edge to the right side of the pants. Align the bottom edge of the waistband to the top edge of the pants, with the right side of the waistband to the right side of the frill. Gather the pants if necessary to adjust the fit. Sew the three layers together (see *figure 6*) and finish the raw edges.

Gather the top edge of the wider frill, as above, until it is the same width as the top of the waistband. With the wrong side of the frill to the right side of the waistband, pin and baste the gathered edge of the frill to the top edge of the waistband. If necessary, gather the top of the waistband to fit the bodice. Slip the seam allowance into the bodice between the lining and the outer fabric, and topstitch all the way around.

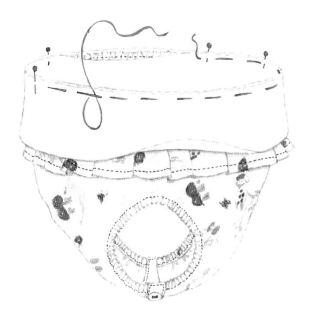

figure 6

Vintage Quilt

A handsewn quilt makes an especially personal gift to mark the birth of a new baby and will be treasured for years to come. It is also a wonderful way to use up scraps of fabrics, as you can mix and match different patterns and colours to great effect. The patches themselves can be hexagons, as here, or diamonds, squares or rectangles. The technique has a rich history in many different cultures and parts of the world, and there are many simple as well as intricate designs from which to take inspiration.

To make a larger quilt, you can either add more rows of hexagonal patches or more strips for the border; alternatively, just increase the width of the borders.

Materials

12–14 different prints, sufficient for 140 hexagonal patches
2 strips of blue print, 88 x 4cm (34¾ x 1½in)
2 strips of blue print, 104 x 4cm (41 x 1½in)
2 strips of dark pink print, 102 x 9cm (40¼ x 3½in)
2 strips of dark pink print, 107 x 9cm (42¼ x 3½in)
2 strips of cream print, 142 x 13.5cm (55¾ x 5¼in)
2 strips of cream print, 102 x 13.5cm (40¼ x 5¼in)
142 x 136cm (55¾ x 53½in) quilting wadding
142 x 136cm (55¾ x 53½in) blue chambray backing fabric
Cream wool yarn and embroidery needle
Card for hexagonal window template
Tracing paper, pencil and fabric pen
Craft knife and cutting mat
Thick backing or freezer paper for patches
Sticky tape
Basting thread
Machine thread
Sewing machine and sewing kit
Iron and ironing board

STEP 1
Making the patches

Trace the hexagonal window template (see page 140) onto card and cut it out with a craft knife. The outer edge of the template is the pattern for the fabric patches and includes a hem allowance; the inner edge is the pattern for the paper backing and is the size of the finished patch.

Lay the template on your fabric and, using a fabric pen, draw around the outer edge of the template, and then cut out the patches with sharp scissors. Cut 140 hexagons from your choice of fabrics, using at least 12–14 different prints.

Fold the backing paper over twice (so you can cut out four shapes at once). Using the template again, trace around the inner edge of the hexagon, then cut out 140 paper patches using a craft knife.

Lay the fabric patches right side down and pin a paper patch to the centre of each. Fold the edges of the fabric over the paper and secure with small pieces of tape. Baste around the edges, then remove the tape (see figure 1). Press the patches with an iron to create crisp edges.

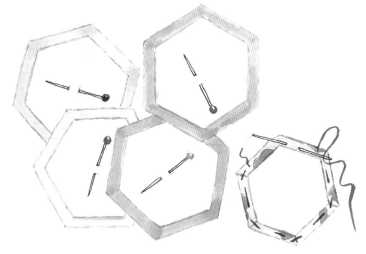

figure 1

STEP 2

Sewing the patchwork

Arrange the patches on the floor in your chosen configuration, making 10 columns and 14 rows.

Starting with a patch in the middle of the second row, join two hexagons together along one edge with overcast stitch: place the patches with right sides together and, using a fine needle and matching thread, pick up a few threads in the edge of both patches, trying not to sew through the paper, and pull through. Repeat neatly along the edge (see figure 2).

Join a third hexagon to the sides of the first two patches in the same way, making sure that they are lined up precisely. Continue until you have attached patches to all six sides of the first hexagon.

Build up the patchwork until you have a rectangular shape, 10 hexagons across and 14 deep.

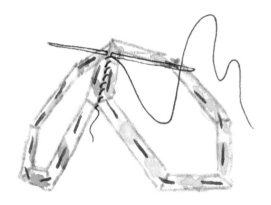

figure 2

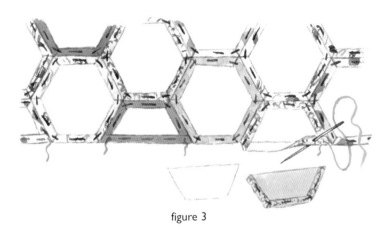

figure 3

STEP 3

Neatening the edges of your patchwork

Lay the patchwork right side down on a flat surface and fold every other patch along the outer edges in half to create straight edges.

Trim the paper backing of these patches along the fold line, and trim the fabric to 1cm (½in) away from the folded line.

Working around the edge of the rectangle, fold the 1cm (½in) of fabric over the edge of the paper and baste it in place (see figure 3).

Remove the basting from the inner edges of the patches, and then press the patchwork.

STEP 4

Adding the borders

Measure the patchwork along both sides and top and bottom, and work out the average length and width. Make the borders as deep as you like, with a 1cm (½in) seam allowance on all sides; if the fabric is not long enough, sew strips together. We made a 2cm- (¾in-) wide blue border, a 7cm- (2¾in-) wide pink border and an 11.5cm- (4½in-) wide cream border.

With right sides together, sew the longer narrow strips to the sides of the patchwork with a 1cm (½in) seam allowance; press the seams open. Join the shorter narrow strips to the top and bottom in the same way. Repeat to join the medium-width border (see figure 4). The widest outer border is joined along the top and bottom first, and then along each side.

Remove the paper backing from the patches.

figure 4

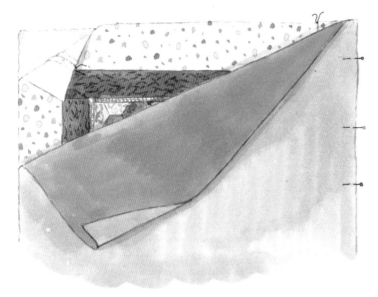

figure 5

STEP 5

Sewing up the wadding and backing fabric

Lay the quilt flat and measure its dimensions. The wadding and backing fabric need to match this size – ours were 142 × 136cm (55¾ × 53½in). If necessary, sew two pieces of fabric together to make the back of the quilt large enough.

Lay the wadding flat and place the patchwork on top of it, right side up. Lay the quilt backing fabric right side down on top of it. Pin and then baste around the edges of the quilt (see figure 5). Using a quilting foot on your sewing machine, sew three-quarters of the way around, with a 1cm (½in) seam allowance.

Clip the corners, and turn the quilt right side out. Turn the seam allowance to the inside along the last quarter of the quilt, and handsew discreetly along the fold to close.

STEP 6

Tying the quilt

Thread an embroidery needle with cream wool yarn. At the corner of every second hexagon, make a couple of stitches through all three layers of the quilt and tie a knot in the yarn. Trim the ends to around 3.5cm (1½in) long (see figure 6). This will ensure that the wadding lies flat.

figure 6

Playtime

From marbles, skipping and the bush-telephone to creative crafting and baking, we treasure our memories of those classic children's pastimes forever. This selection of gorgeous outfits and projects are both practical and fun to wear or use, as well as satisfying to make.

Button-Through Dress

This is a great everyday dress, as it can be worn over jeans or leggings to make it more practical and versatile. It looks as pretty with bare legs and soft pumps for summer-time playing as it does teamed with a long-sleeved T-shirt or a cardigan on colder autumn days.

Cotton voile or poplin are ideal fabrics for a light summer dress, while a soft baby cord is a good option for an autumn version. The contrasting yoke – here in chambray, which looks fresh against the delicate wild-flower print – can lend itself to a number of other fabrics, such as denim, cord or even another print.

Materials

Paper for pattern
75cm (30in) plain chambray for
    yoke, lining and button extensions
1.75m (2yd) printed cotton voile
    for main body of dress and sleeves
6 buttons, 12mm (½in) diameter
1.5m (1¾yd) broderie anglaise trim,
    2.5cm (1in) wide
Basting thread
Matching sewing thread
Sewing machine and sewing kit
Iron and ironing board

STEP 1   figure 1

Making up the yoke

With right sides together, match up the shoulders and pin the front yoke pieces to the back. Sew along the shoulder seams with a 5mm (¼in) seam allowance (see *figure 1*). Repeat for the yoke lining. Press the seams open, then fold and press the bottom of each yoke 5mm (¼in) to the wrong side. With wrong sides together, baste the yoke and lining together around the neckline.

Pin and then baste a length of broderie anglaise trim along the bottom edges of the front yoke pieces. Make sure the right side of the top edge of the trim is facing the wrong side of the bottom edge of the outer front yoke.

figure 2

STEP 2

Making up the body of the dress

With right sides together, sew the two front pieces of the dress to the back piece along the side seams, and finish the raw edges.

Leaving long threads at each end, sew two rows of gathering stitching along the top of the back and front pieces of the dress between the markers, the first row 5mm (¼in) from the edge and the second row 3mm (⅛in) below it. Hold one end of the threads on the same side of the fabric and gather up the material until it is the same width as the bottom of the corresponding yoke pieces. Ease the fabric gently to evenly distribute the gathers.

Push the 8mm (⅜in) seam allowance of the back of the dress into the back yoke, between the outer fabric and the lining, and topstitch along the folded edge (see *figure 2*). Repeat to attach each front panel, making sure the broderie anglaise trim is secured in place when you topstitch.

STEP 3

Making the button extensions and hemming the dress

Fold and press the ends of the button extensions 5mm (¼in) to the wrong side. Press the strips lengthways into thirds, but leave one edge 5mm (¼in) wider than the other. With the right side of the extension to the wrong side of the dress, align the raw edge of one extension with the inside edge of one of the front panels of the dress. Sew with a 5mm (¼in) seam allowance. Flip the folded side of the extension to the outside of the dress, and topstitch down both sides (see *figure 3*). Repeat on the other side of the dress.

Make six vertical buttonholes down the length of the extension on the right of the dress, making the first 1cm (½in) from top and edge, and spacing them approximately 6cm (2⅜in) apart. Sew six corresponding buttons onto the extension on the left of the dress.

To hem the dress, fold and press the bottom edge of the dress 5mm (¼in) to the wrong side. Fold over and press an additional 2cm (¾in) and machine stitch the hem in place.

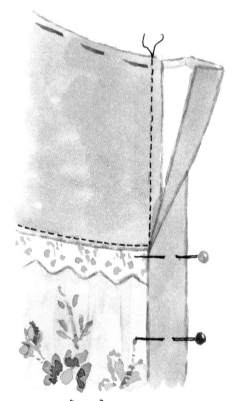

figure 3

figure 4

STEP 4

Making and inserting the sleeves

With right sides together, sew a length of broderie anglaise trim to the bottom of each sleeve, 5mm (¼in) from the edge. Overlock the raw edges, press the seam allowance to the wrong side and topstitch over the fold.

In the same way as you gathered the dress panels (see *step 2*), loosely gather the cap of each sleeve at the shoulder. With right sides together, fit the sleeve into the armhole, aligning the shoulder seam with the centre of the sleeve; sew with 8mm (⅜in) seams. Overlock the raw edges and press the seams towards the yoke.

Fold and press the seam allowance of the armhole below the sleeve to the wrong side. Fold and press all four edges of the seam binding 5mm (¼in) to the wrong side. Starting at the bottom of the yoke, pin the binding onto the inside edge of the armhole and topstitch in place (see *figure 4*). Continue the inner line of topstitching all the way around the armhole, catching the sleeve's overlocked seam allowance in the stitching.

STEP 5

Finishing the neckline

Fold and press the neckline binding in half on the cross grain. Fold and press the ends and one long edge 5mm (¼in) to the wrong side. Align the raw edge of the binding with the edge of the neckline, with the right side of the binding to the inside of the neckline; pin, baste and then machine stitch 5mm (¼in) from the edge.

Flip the folded edge of the binding to the outside of the dress, and topstitch around the neckline (see *figure 5*).

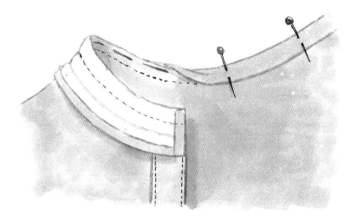

figure 5

STEP 6

Making the pockets

Fold and press the rectangular pocket piece in half lengthways, then press the long edges 5mm (¼in) to the wrong side. Gather the straight edge of the curved pocket piece, so that it fits the width of the rectangular piece. Pin and then baste a length of broderie anglaise trim along this edge and then fit it between the two folded edges of the rectangular piece (see *figure 6*); topstitch along the fold. Press the 5mm (¼in) seam allowance around the raw edge of the pocket to the wrong side.

Make a second pocket in the same way and pin them onto the front of the dress, making sure they are the same distance from the side seams and hem; topstitch around the sides and bottom of each pocket.

figure 6

Dirndl Skirt

Dirndl shapes are adored by little girls, and this skirt, made up of four gathered tiers, is nearly a full circle of fabric, making it wonderful to twirl around in. It looks great with a pretty printed blouse or dressed down with a simple vintage T-shirt. When made up in hardwearing denim, it is as useful as throwing on a pair of jeans, whereas lighter-weight chambray fabric gives it a prettier feel, especially when the hem has been embellished with a pique-edge trim, as shown here. This versatile skirt can also be made in soft, lightweight twills and baby cord, both printed and plain.

Materials

Paper for pattern
1.75m (2yd) plain chambray
7.5m (8¼yd) pique-edge trim,
   1cm (½in) wide
30cm (12in) elastic, 3cm
   (1¼in) wide
Basting thread
Matching sewing thread
Sewing machine and sewing kit
Iron and ironing board

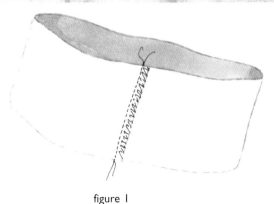

figure 1

STEP 1
Making up the skirt tiers

Join the five strips that make up the fourth (bottom) tier end to end to form one large circle of fabric. With right sides together, pin and baste each piece together in turn, and then machine stitch with 5mm (¼in) seams.

Repeat this process with the three pieces that make up the third tier and the two pieces that make up the second tier. The first tier is made from one long strip, so join this end to end to form a circle, as before (see figure 1). Finish the raw edges of all the seams.

Sugar and spice and all things nice,
That's what little girls are made of.

STEP 2

Building the gathers

Start with the largest, bottom tier. Using a long stitch on the sewing machine and leaving long threads at each end, sew one row of gathering stitching around the top of each tier, 5mm (¼in) from the edge. Sew a second row of gathering stitching 3mm (⅛in) below the first. Hold one end of the threads tightly on the same side of the fabric and gather up the material until it is the same circumference as the bottom of the tier that will be attached above it. Repeat for the two middle tiers (see *figure 2*).

On the top tier, only gather the front half (the back will be elasticated), making the gathered half the same width as half of the finished waistband measurement.

figure 2

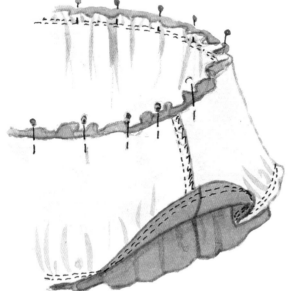

figure 3

STEP 3

Sewing the skirt together

With right sides together, line up the top of the fourth tier with the bottom of the third tier, matching the side seams (see *figure 3*); sew with an 8mm (⅜in) seam allowance.

Attach the top of the third tier to the bottom of the second, and the top of the second to the bottom of the first tier in the same way.

Press the seams upwards, overlock the raw edges, and then topstitch the bottom of the first, second and third tiers.

STEP 4

Making and attaching the waistband

With right sides together, sew the ends of the waistband together, creating a circle. Press the seam open. Fold and press the waistband in half, then open it out and fold and press the top edge 1cm (½in) to the wrong side.

With the right side of the waistband to the wrong side of the skirt, align the raw edges of the waistband and the top tier of the skirt, matching up the seams. Sew them together with a 1cm (½in) seam allowance (see figure 4).

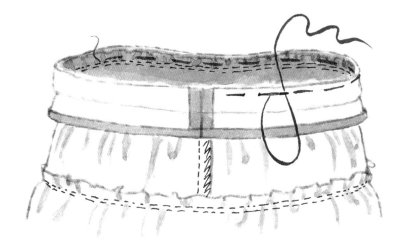

figure 4

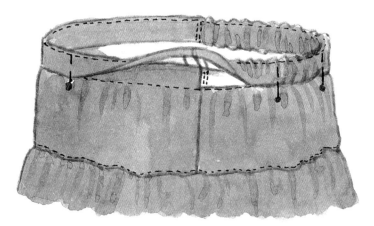

figure 5

STEP 5

Inserting the elastic and finishing the waistband

Cut a length of elastic approximately 10cm (4in) less than the back waistband measurement. Enclose the elastic within the centre fold of the back half of the waistband, butting one end up to the seam. Make sure the elastic overlaps the seam allowance at the top of the skirt, and topstitch the end of the elastic securely into place at the seam.

Topstitch around the waistband along the centre fold, stretching the elastic tight as you sew, so that when it is relaxed the back half of the waistband is gathered and the front half is flat. Topstitch the other end of the elastic in place directly opposite the side seam.

Flip the folded edge of the waistband to the right side of the skirt, over the edge of the elastic (see figure 5). Topstitch all the way along the folded edge, stretching the elastic tight as you sew, as before.

STEP 6

Finishing the hem

To hem the skirt, fold and press the raw edge of the bottom tier 5mm (¼in) to the wrong side. Fold over and press another 5mm (¼in), and machine stitch the hem in place.

Pin the top of the trim along the bottom edge of the hem on the wrong side, so the bottom of the trim overlaps the bottom of the skirt, and topstitch (see figure 6).

figure 6

Dungarees

Dungarees are perfect for toddlers, especially little boys. Worn with a variety of jersey tops and a pair of soft canvas shoes, this practical and appealing garment is a real winner for a hard day's play. These particular ones were inspired by an American pattern from the 1960s.

The dungarees look great made up in any soft baby cord fabric, printed or plain, as well as in classic denim or chambray, and they would be a welcome addition to any kid's wardrobe. For additional detail, you could decorate the bib area with appliqué or use interesting buttons.

Materials

Paper for pattern
1.5m (1¾yd) plain baby cord
2 buttons, 2cm (¾in) diameter
7 buttons, 1cm (⅜in) diameter
40cm (15¾in) elastic, 4cm (1½in) wide
Basting thread
Matching sewing thread
Sewing machine and sewing kit
Iron and ironing board

figure 1

figure 2

STEP 1
Making the two shoulder straps

Pin and baste the front and back of each strip with right sides together, then machine stitch along the long sides and around the V-shaped end. Clip the corners, press the seams open, and turn the straps right side out. Sew two rows of topstitch, one along the edge of the seam and the other 5mm (¼in) in (see figure 1).

Make a vertical buttonhole in each strap, 1.5cm (⅝in) from the point of the V.

STEP 2
Sewing the bib

Pin and baste the front and back of the bib with right sides together, then machine stitch around the top and sides. Clip the corners, press the seams open, and turn the bib right side out. Sew two rows of topstitch, one along the edge of the seam and the other 5mm (¼in) in.

Sew one large button in each of the top corners of the bib, 2cm (¾in) from the side and top (see figure 2).

One, two, three, four, five.
Once I caught a fish alive,
Six, seven, eight, nine ,ten,
Then I let it go again.
Why did you let it go?
Because it bit my finger so.
Which finger did it bite?
This little finger on the right.

STEP 3

Sewing up the bottoms

With right sides together, sew the left and right sides of the bottoms together along the central seams on the front and back of the dungarees, and finish the raw edges (see *figure 3*).

Fold and press the hem of the bottoms 5mm (¼in) to the wrong side, then fold over and press another 3cm (1¼in). Machine stitch along the edge of the hem, then sew another row 5mm (¼in) below the first.

figure 3

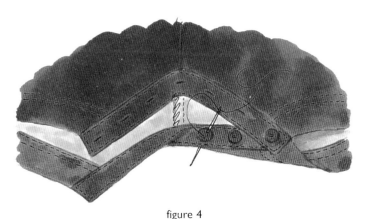

figure 4

STEP 4

Adding the button extensions

Fold and press the ends of the button extensions 5mm (¼in) to the wrong side. Fold and press each strip lengthways into thirds, but leave one edge 5mm (¼in) longer than the other. With the right side of the extension to the wrong side of the bottoms, align the raw edge of the extension with the front of the bottoms and sew 5mm (¼in) in from the edge. Flip the folded edge of the extension to the right side and topstitch all around the edge. Attach the other extension onto the back of the bottoms in the same way.

Make seven horizontal buttonholes along the back extension, one 1cm (½in) from each end and the other three equally spaced between. Sew seven corresponding buttons onto the front button extension (see *figure 4*).

STEP 5

Attaching the bib and straps to the waistband

With right sides together and a 5mm (¼in) seam allowance, sew the ends of the two strips that make up the inside of the waistband together to form a circle. Repeat for the two strips that make up the outside of the waistband. Press the seams open, then fold and press the seam allowance at the top and bottom of both pieces 5mm (¼in) to the wrong side.

On the inside piece, unfold the seam allowance along the top edge, and pin then baste the bottom edge of the bib to the centre front of the inside waistband, with the back of the bib to the right side of the inside waistband.

Pin and baste the shoulder straps to the back of the inside waistband in the same way, making sure that each strap is an equal distance from the side seams (see *figure 5*).

With right sides together, line up the top raw edges of the inside and outside waistbands; pin and baste in place. Machine stitch all the way around, 5mm (¼in) from the edge, sewing the inner and outer waistbands together, with the bib and straps secured between the two layers.

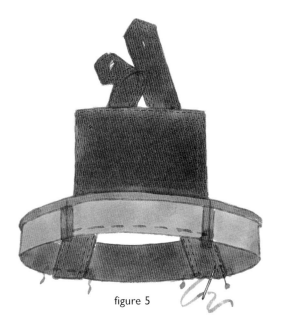

figure 5

STEP 6
Fitting the elastic

Machine stitch one end of the elastic to the inside portion of the waistband at one side of the bib. Butting the piece of elastic up to the seam at the top of the waistband, topstitch the top and bottom edges of elastic in place, stretching it tight as you sew, so that the elastic reaches all the way along the inside waistband to the other side of the bib (the fabric will gather up when the elastic is relaxed) (see figure 6). Stitch the other end of the elastic in place.

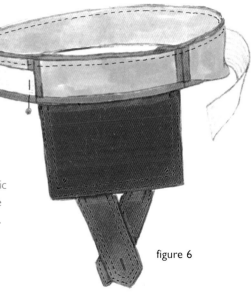

figure 6

STEP 7
Attaching the bottoms

Starting from one of the notches that will align with the edge of the bib, sew two rows of gathering stitching around the back of the bottoms to the other notch. Using a long stitch on the sewing machine and leaving long threads at both ends, sew the first row 5mm (¼in) in from the edge and the second row 3mm (⅛in) below the first. Hold the ends of the threads tightly on top of the fabric and gather until the bottoms fit the waistband with the elastic fully stretched. The front of the bottoms, which will be directly below the bib, remains ungathered (see figure 7).

Turn the waistband right side out and align the bottom edge of the inside waistband with the gathered edge of the dungarees bottoms, with the right side of the waistband to the wrong side of the bottoms. Make sure the central front and back seams of the bottoms align with the centre front and back of the waistband, then pin and baste in place.

figure 7

STEP 8
Finishing the waistband

Flip the folded bottom edge of the outer waistband down and pin it in place over the gathered edge of the dungarees bottoms, so the bottoms are sandwiched between the inside and outside portions of the waistband. Topstitch all the way along the folded edge, securing all the layers together, pulling the elastic tight as you sew.

Topstitch along the top edge of the non-elasticated portion of the waistband, beneath the bib, then topstitch a rectangle around this area, 5mm (¼in) in (see figure 8).

figure 8

Frogs and snails and puppy-dogs' tails,
That's what little boys are made of.

Madras-Check Shorts

These are a classic shape for boys' shorts, with a tie waist and a leg length to just below the knee. Making them up in a Madras cotton check, such as the one we used here, ensures that they maintain a vintage feel. Alternative fabrics could include soft, lightweight denims and printed or plain cotton poplins.

Teamed with a retro T-shirt and soft canvas boots, these shorts are a great playtime garment for any little boy. If you wish, you could make the leg length shorter, or make them full length for a pair of casual lightweight summer trousers.

Materials

Paper for pattern
1.75m (2yd) Madras cotton
  check
18cm (7in) zip
Basting thread
Matching sewing thread
Sewing machine and sewing kit
Iron and ironing board
Safety pin

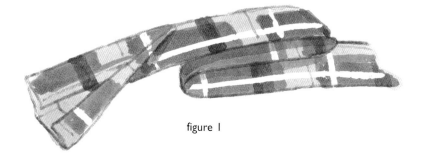

figure 1

STEP 1

Making the drawstring

Fold and press both ends of the drawstring 1cm (½in) to the wrong side, then fold and press the strip in half lengthways. Open it out and press both raw edges into the centre fold, and then fold and press it in half again, so that the strip is in four layers (see *figure 1*). Topstitch all the way around.

STEP 2

Making and attaching the pockets

Fold the pocket in half with wrong sides together and sew along the bottom with a 5mm (¼in) seam. Turn the pocket inside out and topstitch along the bottom seam, enclosing the seam allowance.

Fold and press the edges of the pocket flap 5mm (¼in) to the wrong side. Fold and press the diagonal edge of the front piece of the shorts 5mm (¼in) to the wrong side. Position the pocket flap on the front piece of the shorts with the wrong side of the flap to the right side of the shorts. Pin and baste in place, then topstitch two rows around the four outer sides of the pocket flap, the first row along the edge and a second row 5mm (¼in) in.

Fold and press the diagonal edge of the pocket 5mm (¼in) to the wrong side. Align the folded diagonal edges of the pocket and the front piece of the shorts, and pin (see *figure 2*). Topstitch one row along the edge and another row 5mm (¼in) in.

Baste the pocket and shorts together at the waist.

With right sides together, sew the front and back pieces of the shorts together along the side seams. Press the seams towards the back of the shorts; overlock the raw edges and topstitch along the fold of the seams and 5mm (¼in) in.

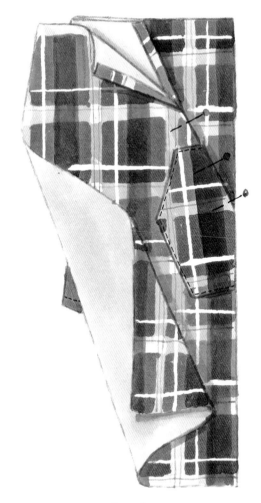

figure 2

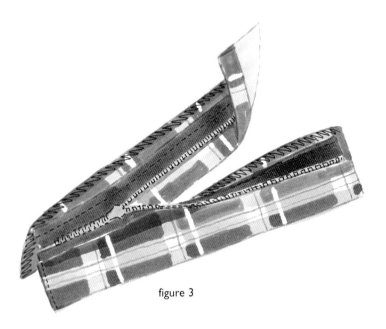

figure 3

STEP 3

Preparing the zip

Fold the rectangular piece of the zipper guard in half with wrong sides together, and machine stitch along the bottom end. Turn the piece right side out and topstitch along the seam, enclosing the seam allowance.

Pin and baste the left side (as you look at it) of the zipper tape 5mm (¼in) from the raw edge of the rectangular strip.

With right sides together, pin and baste the strip of fabric with the curved side to the other side of the zipper tape. Fold and press the straight edge of the curved strip 5mm (¼in) to the wrong side. Machine stitch the zipper tapes in place using the zipper foot on your sewing machine. Overlock the raw edges (see *figure 3*).

STEP 4
Making the fly

Fold and press the edge of the left front piece of the shorts 5mm (¼in) to the wrong side. Match the folded portion of the fly with the folded edge of the zipper guard (see *figure 4*). Open the zip and topstitch along the edge of the fold. From the inside, topstitch two rows, 5mm (¼in) apart, along the curve of the zipper guard up to the waistband.

Fold and press the edge of the right front piece 5mm (¼in) to the wrong side. Pin and baste the fold onto the right zipper tape, clipping into the seam allowance at the bottom of the tape. Machine stitch in place and overlock the raw edge.

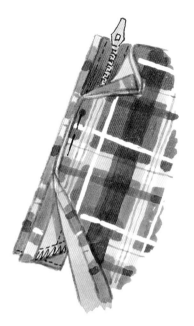

figure 4

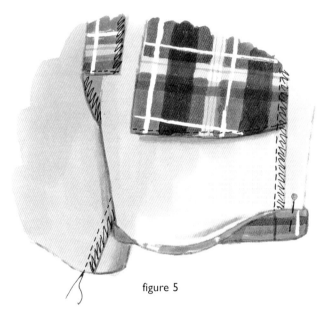

figure 5

STEP 5
Sewing up the shorts

Sew the left and right sides of the shorts together down the centre front and back seams, starting at the crotch and sewing up to the fly at the front and the waistband at the back. Press the seam allowance to the right, overlock the raw edges and topstitch over the seam allowance.

With right sides together, sew the front of the shorts to the back forming the inside leg seams. Finish the raw edges.

Fold and press the bottom edges of each leg 5mm (¼in) to the wrong side. Fold over and press an additional 2.5cm (1in), and machine stitch the hems (see *figure 5*).

STEP 6
Fashioning the waistband

With right sides together and a 5mm (¼in) seam allowance, sew the ends of the waistband together to form a circle. Fold and press the waistband in half with wrong sides together, and then fold and press the bottom front edge 5mm (¼in) to the wrong side.

At the centre front of the waistband, make two vertical buttonholes approximately 6cm (2⅜in) apart for the drawstring.

Align the raw edges of the waistband and the shorts, with the right side of the waistband to the wrong side of the shorts, and sew them together 5mm (¼in) from the edge.

Flip the folded edge of the waistband to the right side of the shorts and topstitch in place; then topstitch along the top edge of the waistband.

Using a safety pin, thread the drawstring through the waistband (see *figure 6*).

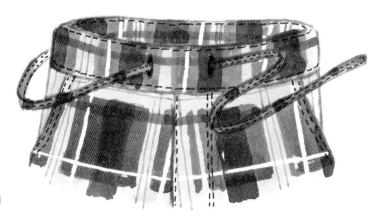

figure 6

Classic Shirt

The classic shape of this shirt lends itself perfectly to plain or printed fine-grade cotton poplins, as well as gingham and larger checked fabrics. It is a staple piece for any boy's wardrobe and can be worn with a T-shirt underneath to remove the formal connotations of a button-through shirt.

Using a conversational print, such as the Pirate one shown here, is a great way to give the shirt a point of difference, while sourcing interesting buttons to use is another way to add unique detail. This Pirate print, for instance, would look great teamed with some old buttons depicting anchors – a popular vintage button design and not hard to find.

Materials

Paper for pattern
2.25m (2½yd) printed cotton
   poplin
10 buttons, 1cm (⅜in) diameter
Basting thread
Matching sewing thread
Sewing machine and sewing kit
Iron and ironing board

figure 1

STEP 1

Starting the bodice

Align the top of the yoke lining with the top of the front bodice pieces, with the right side of the yoke lining to the wrong side of the front bodices, and pin and baste. With right sides together, pin the top of the outer yoke to the top of the front bodice pieces, then machine stitch along the shoulder seams 5mm (¼in) from the edge. Flip the right side of the outer yoke to the back, so the wrong sides of the yoke and lining are together with the seam allowance between; press, and then topstitch along the fold of the shoulder seam and 5mm (¼in) away from it, securing the yoke and lining together.

Align the top edge of the back bodice with the bottom edge of the yoke lining, with the wrong side of the bodice to the right side of the lining. Sew with a 5mm (¼in) seam allowance. Press the seam allowance up towards the yoke.

Fold and press the bottom edge of the outer yoke 5mm (¼in) to the wrong side. Align the folded bottom edge of the outer yoke with the seam on the back bodice; pin and baste, then topstitch along the folded edge and 5mm (¼in) above the seam (see figure 1).

Pin and baste the yoke and lining together along the back neckline.

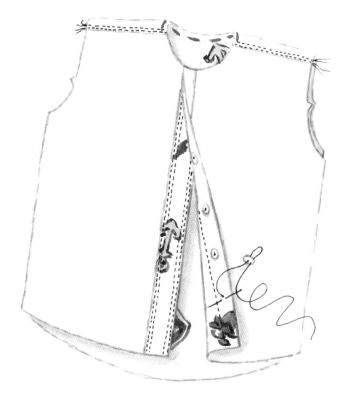

figure 2

STEP 2
Making the button plackets

The button placket on the left of the shirt is narrower than the buttonhole placket on the right.

For the button placket, fold and press the central edge of the left (as you look at it) front bodice 1cm (½in) to the wrong side. Fold over and press another 2cm (¾in), then machine stitch close to the folded edge.

For the buttonhole placket, fold and press the central edge of the right front bodice 2cm (¾in) to the wrong side. Fold over and press another 3cm (1¼in). Machine stitch along both folded edges and then topstitch two more lines 5mm (¼in) inside the first lines.

Make five vertical buttonholes in the wider placket centrally between the rows of topstitching. Make the first 4.5cm (1¾in) from the seam allowance at the top and space the other four approximately 6cm (2⅜in) apart. Sew corresponding buttons onto the narrower placket (see figure 2).

STEP 3
Creating the collar

With right sides together, sew the sides and top of the collar pieces together with a 5mm (¼in) seam allowance. Turn the collar right side out and press, then topstitch around the seam and 5mm (¼in) in from it.

Align the top curved edges of the collar extensions with the raw bottom edges of the collar, with the right side of one extension to the right sides of the collar, one extension on each side of the collar, and the collar positioned centrally between the curved ends of the extension (see figure 3). Sew along the curved sides and top of the collar extension with a 5mm (¼in) seam allowance. Clip the seam allowance at the curves and then turn the collar extension right side out and press.

Fold and press the bottom edge of the inner collar extension 5mm (¼in) to the wrong side. With right sides together, align the raw edge of the outer collar extension to the neckline of the shirt and sew 5mm (¼in) from the edge. Flip the folded edge of the inner collar extension to the inside of the neckline and topstitch along the edge and around the collar extension.

Make a horizontal buttonhole in the right end of the collar extension, 5mm (¼in) from the edge and 1cm (½in) above the seam at the bottom. Sew a corresponding button on the left end of the collar extension.

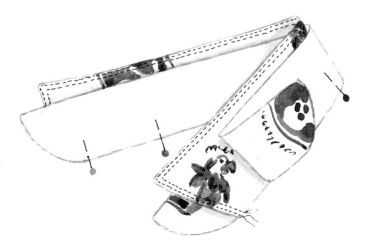

figure 3

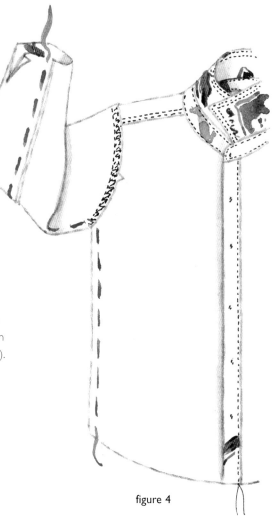

figure 4

STEP 4

Adding the sleeves

With right sides together, match the notches on the sleeve with the bodice and sew with a 5mm (¼in) seam allowance. Press the seam allowance towards the bodice, overlock the raw edges, then topstitch two rows, one along the fold of the seam and one along the edge of the seam allowance.

Starting at the cuff and with right sides together, pin and baste the two sides of the sleeve together, and continue from the armhole down the bodice, joining the front to the back at the side seam (see figure 4). Machine stitch along the seam allowance, then press the seam to one side and overlock the raw edges. Repeat on the other side.

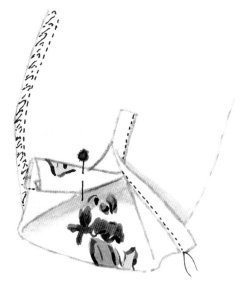

figure 5

STEP 5

Making the cuff laps

Fold and press one cuff lap into thirds, but leave one edge 5mm (¼in) longer than the other. Align the right side of the raw edge of the lap with the inside of the lower slit in the sleeve and sew with a 5mm (¼in) seam allowance. Flip the folded side of the lap to the outside of the sleeve and topstitch the edge.

Fold and press the ends of the other cuff lap 5mm (¼in) to the wrong side. Fold and press the lap into thirds, but leave one edge 5mm (¼in) longer than the other. Align the raw edge of the right side of the lap with the inside of the upper slit in the sleeve (the lap extends beyond the cuff opening in the sleeve), and sew with a 5mm (¼in) seam allowance. Flip the folded side of the lap to the outside of the sleeve (see figure 5), and fold and press the overlapping end into a V-shape. Topstitch along the edge of the lap, around the V-shape at the end and across the lap extension to secure.

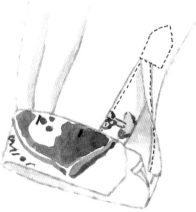

STEP 6

figure 6

Finishing the cuffs

Make two tucks on the edge of the sleeves at the notches, and tack.

With right sides together, fold and press the cuff in half. Sew the V-shaped end with a 5mm (¼in) seam allowance, from the fold to 5mm (¼in) from the raw edge. Turn the cuff right side out and press; fold and press the straight end and the outer bottom edge 5mm (¼in) to the wrong side.

Align the right side of the raw edge of the cuff with the inside of the sleeve, with the V-shaped end of the cuff to the upper lap extension; sew with a 5mm (¼in) seam allowance. Flip the folded side of the cuff to the outside of the sleeve and pin (see figure 6). Topstitch two rows, one around the edge of the cuff and one 5mm (¼in) in from the first.

Make a horizontal buttonhole in the middle of the V-shaped end. Sew two buttons on the other side of the cuff, the first just in from the inner row of topstitching and the second 2cm (¾in) further in from the first.

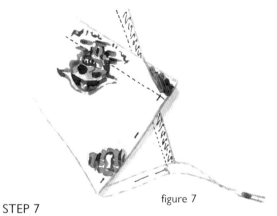

STEP 7

figure 7

Finishing the shirt

Fold the bottom edge of the shirt 5mm (¼in) to the wrong side and press. Fold over and press the hem another 5mm (¼in), then sew all the way around (see figure 7).

Bush Telephones

What You Need – An adult to help • Two metal cans (clean and dry, and with no sharp edges) • Skewer to punch hole • 3–3.5m (10–12ft) of thin string, such as kite string or nylon string

What You Do – Punch a hole in the centre of the base of each can, just large enough for the string to go through. From the outside, thread one end of the string through the hole in one can. Tie a couple of knots in the end of the string so that it will not slip back through when pulled tight. Do the same with the other end of the string using the other can.

With one person holding each can, stretch the string so that it is tight. One person talking into one can sends vibrations through the tightened string to the other can. The person with their ear to the other can will be able to hear what was said.

Marbles

1 Draw or mark out a circle 60–90cm (2–3ft) in diameter. (Use chalk on concrete, a stick in dirt, or a piece of string on indoor floors.)

2 Select your 'shooter' and place your 'target marbles' inside the circle; the other players do the same. The shooter should be larger than the target marbles – it is the designated marble used to knock targets out of the ring.

3 Take your turn by shooting your marble from outside the ring at any marble inside the ring. Shoot by kneeling on the ground and flicking your marble out of your fist with your thumb.

4 Collect any marbles you've knocked out of the ring and then shoot again. If you haven't knocked any marbles out and/or your shooter remains in the ring, let the next player shoot.

5 Continue shooting in turn until the ring is empty. Whoever has the most marbles wins.

Cover-All Apron

This useful piece is based on the old-fashioned tabard-style apron, which is much more practical for covering 'more kid' than the average apron shape. It's a great cover-up for baking as well as messy art sessions that all kids love, involving modelling clay and pot paints. The other use is, of course, for really messy eaters at the dinner table.

The perfect fabric for this apron is a wipe-clean oilcloth, which looks especially charming in vintage-inspired prints. The cotton binding provides a colourful contrast.

Materials

Paper for pattern
1m (40in) printed oilcloth
4.5m (5yd) double-folded bias
    binding (or you can make
    your own in contrasting
    cotton fabric by cutting
    strips on the bias using the
    pattern pieces provided)
Basting thread
Matching sewing thread
Sewing machine and sewing kit

figure 1

STEP 1

Constructing the apron

With right sides together, sew the front and back pieces together at the shoulders (see *figure 1*). Turn the apron right side out.

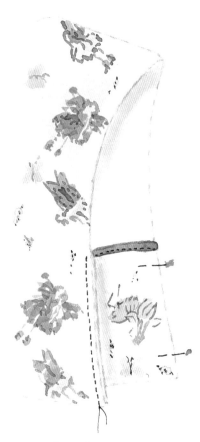

figure 2

STEP 2

Adding the side panels

Encase the top edge of each side panel in bias binding, pushing the edge of the fabric into the centre fold, and topstitch.

Align the bottom of the side panels with the bottom outside edge of the front and back bodice. With wrong sides together, pin and then machine stitch the side panels to the bodice (see *figure 2*).

STEP 3

The pocket

Push the top edge of the pocket into the centre fold of the bias binding; pin and then topstitch.

With the right side of the apron to the wrong side of the pocket, pin the pocket onto the front of the apron, aligning the bottom edges and side seams (see *figure 3*). Sew the pocket in place along the sides and bottom.

figure 3

figure 4

STEP 4

Finishing the seams

Starting at the bottom of one front side seam and working around the armhole and down to the bottom of the back side seam, encase the raw edges of the apron with the bias binding, pushing the material into the centre fold; pin and then topstitch. Repeat on the other side of the apron.

Repeat this process, beginning at the top of one side of the back opening and working down the centre and around the bottom edge, pushing the side seams flat, and then all the way up the other centre back edge to the neckline.

Sew bias binding around the neckline of the apron in the same way, but this time leaving 14cm (5½in) of loose bias binding at either end to make the tie fastenings. Continue the topstitching along the edge of the bias binding ties.

Cut two 14cm- (5½in-) lengths of bias binding and topstitch along the edges. Hand-stitch the end of one tie to the inside of the apron halfway down each side of the back (see *figure 4*).

Simple Shortbread Cookies

175g (6oz) plain flour
175g (6oz) butter
5 tablespoons caster sugar

If you want to be a little creative and healthy, replace the caster sugar with sticky brown sugar; use 25g (1oz) less flour and add oats, chopped nuts, raisins or chocolate chips, or a combination. Have a few goes and come up with your own special recipe.

1 Preheat the oven to 150°C/300°F/gas mark 2.
2 Blend all the ingredients well. The dough will be stiff.
3 Sprinkle your work surface with flour to prevent the dough from sticking, and press or roll out with a rolling pin and use cookie cutters to cut into shapes.
4 Place on a buttered baking tray and bake for approximately 30 minutes, until pale golden brown on the edges.
5 Allow to cool and dust with icing sugar.

Boy's Short-Sleeved Shirt

This classic American retro shape, with a boxy body, revere collar and short sleeves, makes such a cute summer shirt for little boys and looks great teamed with a pair of chino shorts or classic blue denim jeans.

The shirt lends itself to Hawaiian-type prints or interesting conversational prints, such as the aeroplane one we have used, in a good grade cotton poplin. For smaller sizes, it may be worth scouring vintage fairs and markets for man-size retro shirts in this classic style, which can be cut up and reused – there is a treasure-trove of fabulous prints to be found on men's shirts from the 1950s, 1960s and 1970s.

Materials

Paper for pattern
1.4m (1½yd) printed cotton
    poplin
5 buttons, 1cm (⅜in) diameter
Basting thread
Matching sewing thread
Sewing machine and sewing kit
Iron and ironing board

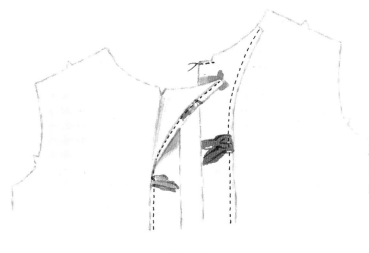

figure 1

STEP 1

Making the button plackets

Hem the centre edges of the front bodice pieces by folding and pressing the raw edges 5mm (¼in) to the wrong side, then folding and pressing another 5mm (¼in) and machine stitching in place.

Fold the centre edges of the front bodices to the wrong side along the 3.5cm (1⅜in) fold lines, and press. Fold and press the seam allowance at the top edge of the button plackets 5mm (¼in) to the wrong side. Clip into the material at the point where the collar will start, and topstitch along the folded edge from the outer corner of the plackets to the point where the collar will start (see figure 1).

Make five vertical buttonholes on the right-hand placket (as you look at the shirt). Position the first buttonhole 3cm (1¼in) from the top and 1cm (½in) from the centre edge, and space the other four approximately 5cm (2in) apart. Sew corresponding buttons on the left-hand placket. The buttons and buttonholes will keep the plackets in place.

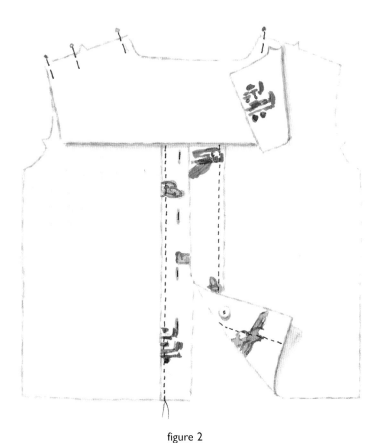

figure 2

STEP 2

Constructing the yoke and front bodice

Pin and then baste the yoke lining and the front bodice pieces together at the shoulders, with the right side of the lining to the wrong side of the front bodice (see *figure 2*).

With right sides together, align the outer yoke with the front bodice pieces at the shoulders and sew with a 5mm (¼in) seam allowance.

Flip the outer yoke and front bodice right sides out and press the yoke and lining to the back, then topstitch over the fold 5mm (¼in) from the shoulder seam.

STEP 3

Attaching the back bodice

Make two tucks on the top of the back bodice at the notches, and tack.

Lay the yoke on your work surface with the right side of the outer yoke facing down. Bring the bottom edges of the yoke and the yoke lining up through the yoke, between the lining and the outer layer, and out through the gap at the neckline. With the back bodice wrong side up, feed the top edge through the gap in the neckline, between the lining and the outer yoke. Sew all three edges together with a 5mm (¼in) seam allowance.

Pull the back bodice back down through the bottom of the yoke. Press the seam flat and then machine stitch over the seam allowance (see *figure 3*).

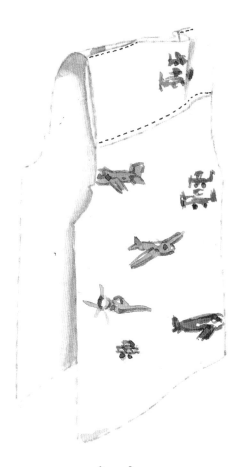

figure 3

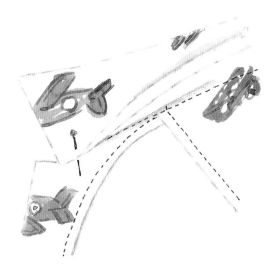

figure 4

STEP 4
Creating the collar

With right sides together, sew the front and back pieces of the collar together along the sides and top with a 5mm (¼in) seam allowance. Turn the collar right side out and press. Fold and press the bottom edge of the front of the collar 5mm (¼in) to the wrong side.

With right sides together, sew the back of the collar onto the back of the bodice with a 5mm (¼in) seam allowance. Press the seam upwards, and pin the folded edge of the front of the collar to the inside of the shirt (see *figure 4*); topstitch along the fold. Then topstitch along the sides and top of the collar 5mm (¼in) from the edge.

STEP 5
Making the cuffs

Fold and press the bottom end of each sleeve 2.5cm (1in) to the wrong side and topstitch 5mm (¼in) from the fold.

Lay the sleeve right side up and make a 5mm- (¼in-) wide horizontal pleat 1.5cm (⅝in) above the bottom edge (see *figure 5*); machine stitch in place and then press the fold towards the crown of the sleeve.

figure 5

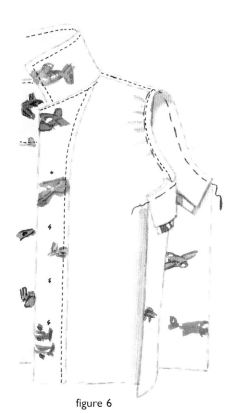

figure 6

STEP 6
Inserting the sleeves

Using a long stitch length on the sewing machine, sew a row of gathering stitching 5mm (¼in) in along the curve of the armhole. Match the notches on the sleeve with the bodice and sew the sleeves in place with a 5mm (¼in) seam allowance, sewing over the gathering stitching (see *figure 6*). Press the seam towards the bodice, overlock the raw edges and topstitch over the seam allowance all the way around the armhole.

STEP 7

Sewing up the sleeves and side seams

Starting at the cuff, pin along the length of the sleeves and side seams of the bodice. Machine stitch with a 1cm (½in) seam allowance, stopping 8cm (3in) from the bottom of the shirt to form the side pleats (see *figure 7*).

Press the seam to one side and overlock the raw edges to about 3cm (1¼in) above the pleat. Sew zigzag stitching along the raw edges of the pleat, then fold each side 5mm (¼in) to the wrong side and topstitch in place.

Hem the bottom of the shirt by folding and pressing 5mm (¼in) to the wrong side. Fold over and press another 2.5cm (1in) and machine stitch in place.

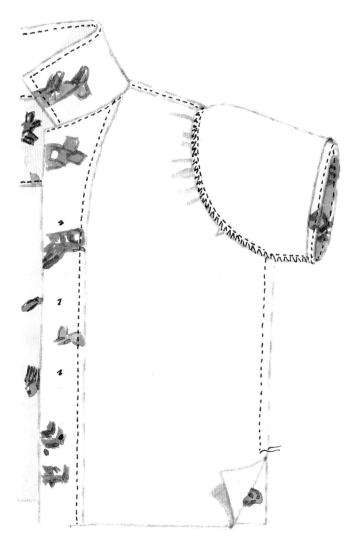

figure 7

figure 8

STEP 8

Adding the pocket

Fold and press the top of the pocket 2.5cm (1in) to the wrong side and topstitch 5mm (¼in) from the fold. Fold over and press the top of the pocket another 2.5cm (1in) and topstitch 5mm (¼in) from the fold. Press the folded portion to the right side of the pocket (see *figure 8*).

Sew zigzag stitch along the raw edges of the pocket, then fold and press both sides and the bottom of the pocket 5mm (¼in) to the wrong side.

Topstitch the pocket onto the left-hand front of the shirt, positioning it 7cm (2¾in) from the centre edge and 4.5cm (1¾in) from the hem.

Easy Paper Planes

1 Fold a sheet of paper exactly in half lengthways, and reopen it so you have a crease separating the two halves.

2 On one end of the paper, fold each corner in towards the centre to the point where the inside edges butt up to the centre crease.

3 Starting at the very tip of the point, fold the paper down on each side so the inside edges line up with the centre crease.

4 Turn the paper plane over and fold it in half along the centre crease.

5 Fold the first wing with the line of the fold running nearly parallel to the centre line of the plane. Make this fold from 1–2cm (½–¾in) from the centre.

6 Fold the second wing exactly as you did the first.

Your plane may need some fine-tuning before it will fly perfectly straight. If it dives, slightly angle the rear of the wings up. If it climbs and crashes, slightly angle the rear of the wings down.

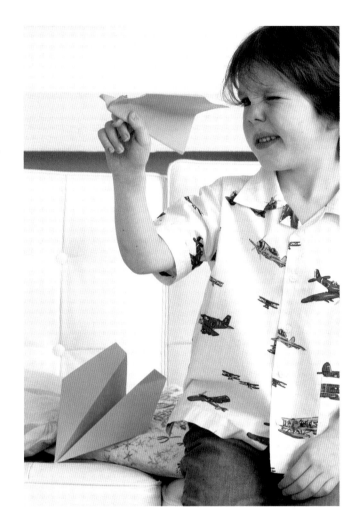

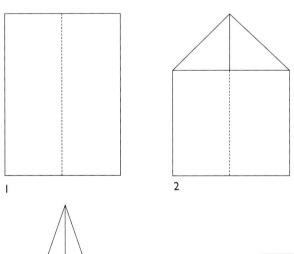

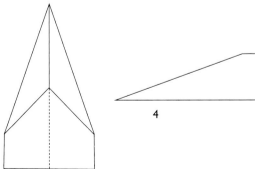

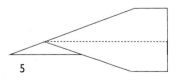

Notice Board

Adding a charming decorative touch to a child's room, this practical and attractive notice board is a great way to keep a record of their party invites, birthday cards and treasured photos. Gorgeous vintage-style fabrics have been used to cover the front of the boards, with plain fabric on the back for a neat finish. Lengths of elastic are crisscrossed over the board to keep the pictures in place – making finger-pricking pins redundant. You don't have to use wadding, but it ensures that the pictures are held extra-snugly beneath the elastic. Choose a vintage ribbon to hang the notice board, perhaps in a stripe or a plain contrasting colour.

Materials

Wooden board, 50 x 35cm
(19¾ x 13¾in)
70g (2oz), 5–7mm- (¼in-) thick
wadding, 50 x 35cm (19¾ x 13¾in)
Printed cotton 66 x 51cm (26 x 20in)
Plain fabric, 52 x 37cm (21 x 14½in)
3.2m (3½yd) elastic, 1cm (½in) wide
50cm (19¾in) ribbon, 1cm (½in) wide
Tape measure, scissors and pins
Hot-glue gun and glue
Staple gun and staples
Iron and ironing board

figure 1

STEP 1

Covering the board

Trim the wadding to the same size as your wooden board and attach it to one side of the board with a few dabs of glue.

Cut a rectangle of fabric 16cm (6¼in) larger than your board on both dimensions. Press the fabric and lay it on your work surface wrong side up. Lay the board in the centre of the fabric, wadding side down. Make sure you have an equal overlap of fabric (of 8cm/3in) all the way around the board.

Starting in the centre of one long side, fold the edge of the fabric over the board, and secure it in place on the back with a dab of glue and a staple. Stretch the fabric taut from the opposite side, and glue and staple in place. Continue around the board, working outwards from the centre and alternating sides to ensure an even tension all over. At each corner, make a triangular fold by folding the loose fabric up to the top edge and then back on itself (see *figure 1*). Staple the fold in place.

STEP 2

Adding the elastic

Measure and mark with pins three equally spaced points along the top and bottom of the board, approximately 12cm (4¾in) apart, measuring from the left-hand corner.

Cut eight 40cm (15½in) lengths of elastic. Secure one end of the first piece on the back of the board at the top left corner by stapling it in place. Take the elastic diagonally over the front of the board to the first pin on the bottom edge, and staple the other end to the back of the board. Position the next piece parallel to the first, taking it from the first pin on the top edge to the second pin on the bottom edge. Continue in this way, and then work back in the other direction to crisscross the lengths of elastic, taking the fifth piece diagonally from the top right corner to the last pin on the bottom left edge (see *figure 2*).

To hang the notice board, cut a length of ribbon approximately 50cm (19¾in) long and staple one end at each corner on the back of the board.

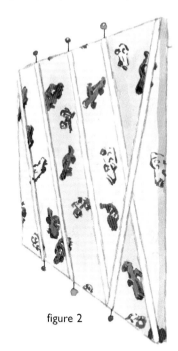

figure 2

STEP 3

Finishing the back of the board

Cut another piece of fabric 1cm (½in) larger than the board all the way round. Fold and press the raw edges 1cm (½in) to the wrong side. Glue the piece of fabric to the back of the board (see *figure 3*).

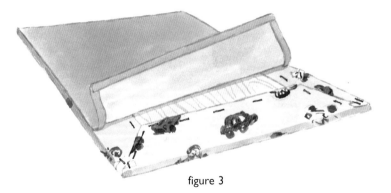

figure 3

Beanbag Frog

Small toys made from vintage fabrics not only make great playthings for little ones but also add a special touch to a child's room. It is a charming way to use up smaller scraps of cloth left over from other projects, or to reinvent a much-loved fabric, such as a favourite dress that no longer fits or a vintage scarf or shirt. As with the Tooth Fairy Pillow (see page 136), if a toy is made up in a special fabric it will hold even more childhood nostalgia.

This lovely frog shape came from a 1970s pattern. It is a very easy but rewarding project, and the beanbag frog is a lovely toy for your child to keep.

Materials

Tracing paper, pencil and scissors
Paper for frog pattern
40cm (15¾in) printed cotton
    or baby cord
Beanbag filling
2 buttons, 1.5cm (⅝in) diameter
    (or embroidery thread) for eyes
Small funnel
Basting thread
Matching sewing thread
Sewing machine and sewing kit
Iron and ironing board

STEP 1
Starting the frog

Trace the template on page 140 onto paper and cut out the pattern. Cut out the front and back of the frog.

With right sides together, sew the front and back pieces together with a 5mm (¼in) seam allowance, starting at the bottom of the inside left leg. Stop sewing opposite your starting point, on the inside right leg, leaving a gap of 2.5–5cm (1–2in). Snip into the seam allowance on the curved parts of the frog (see figure 1), then press the seams open.

figure 1

STEP 2
Filling the frog

Turn the fabric right side out. Holding the frog upside down, insert the end of a funnel into the opening and fill the frog with beanbag filling. Tuck the seam allowance to the inside of the opening, and neatly hand-stitch to close (see figure 2).

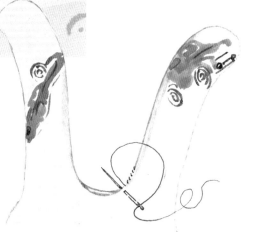

figure 2

STEP 3
Adding the eyes

Give the frog two button eyes, sewing one very securely onto each side of the head using two strands of thread (see figure 3). Alternatively, you can embroider the eyes using silk embroidery thread.

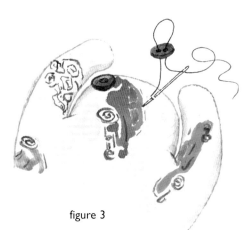

figure 3

Parties

Who doesn't remember their favourite childhood party outfit? Whether your child is set for a tea party in Wonderland or an adventure in the Wild West, this magical and nostalgic selection will thrill even the pickiest Alice or Arkansas Tom.

Full-Circle Dress

The inspiration for the design of this stunning dress was a vintage find from Portobello Market. The most appealing part of the original dress was the amazing full-circle skirt, which little girls love to twirl around in. The design translates well into different fabrics, from soft cotton voiles in pretty florals or gingham checks for spring/summer to baby cords for autumn/winter.

This dress has been one of our best-sellers for the past few years throughout both seasons. A really versatile garment, it looks great layered with a T-shirt and cardigan and teamed with sheepskin boots for a cosy winter look, or with nothing more than sandals and a daisy chain.

Materials

Paper for pattern
4.25m (4¾yd) printed cotton
4 buttons, 12mm (½in) diameter
Basting thread
Matching sewing thread
Sewing machine and sewing kit
Iron and ironing board

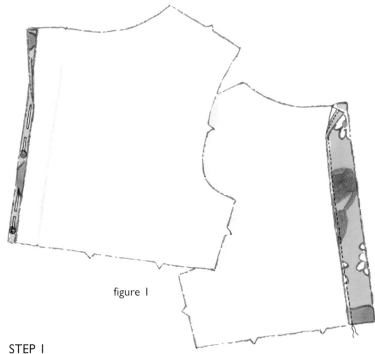

figure 1

STEP 1

Making the back button plackets

Fold and press the centre edge of the left and right back bodices 5mm (¼in) to the wrong side. Fold over and press another 5mm (¼in) and machine stitch the hems in place. To form the plackets, fold wrong sides together at the fold line, and press (see *figure 1*). Sew a couple of tacks at the top and bottom to hold the plackets in place.

STEP 2

Attaching the waistband to the bodice

With right sides together, match up the inner and outer back waistband pieces and sew them together along one end with a 5mm (¼in) seam allowance. Press the seams open.

Insert the back right bodice between the two layers of the back right waistband, matching the notches and butting up the fold of the placket to the seam at the end of the waistband. Make sure that the right side of the outer waistband is to the right side of the back bodice. Sew the three layers together along the bottom edge with a 5mm (¼in) seam allowance. Trim off the inside corner where the waistband joins the placket, and press the waistband downwards so wrong sides are together (see *figure 2*). Topstitch along the top edge of the waistband. Repeat to attach the back left waistband and bodice.

Sew the inner and outer layers of the front waistband to the front bodice piece in the same way.

figure 2

STEP 3

Making the tie belt

With right sides together, matching the notches, sew the tie belt pieces together along both long sides and one end with a 5mm (¼in) seam allowance, leaving the other end open.

Turn the belts right side out through the open end, and press. Topstitch along the fold of the seams.

Pin and baste the open end of the tie belt to the sides of the left and right back bodices, aligning the top edge of the ties with the top of the waistband (see *figure 3*).

figure 3

figure 4

STEP 4

Sewing the bodice together

With right sides together, matching the notches, pin the front bodice to the back bodices at the shoulder and side seams. The tie belt will be secured in place when you sew along the seam allowance, so make sure the lengths are on the inside between the layers (see *figure 4*). Finish the raw edges.

STEP 5

Sewing on the neck and arm bindings

Fold the neck binding (which is cut on the bias) in half lengthways along the fold line, and press. Pin the binding to the right side of the neckline, aligning the raw edges and extending the ends of the binding 5mm (¼in) beyond the centre back edges (see *figure 5*). Machine stitch 5mm (¼in) from the raw edge, easing the binding to fit as you sew.

Press the binding towards the neck, and press the seam towards the binding. Turn the pressed edge of the binding to the inside, so that it encases the raw edges and just covers the line of stitching. Topstitch in place, easing the binding to fit as you sew.

Turn in the ends of the binding at the back of the neck, and press. Topstitch over the binding and down the back opening to the top of the waistband, close to the edge.

Press one long edge of each arm binding 5mm (¼in) to the wrong side. Sew the ends of the arm bindings together to make two circles, and press the seams open. Align the raw edges of the bindings with the armholes, right sides together. Sew with a 5mm (¼in) seam allowance, then turn the folded edge of the bindings to the inside of the armholes and topstitch in place.

figure 5

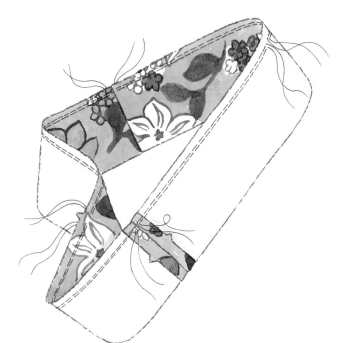

figure 6

STEP 6

Making up the first layer of the skirt

Sew the front and back sections of the first layer of the skirt together along the seam allowance at the side seams to form a circle.

Using a long stitch on the sewing machine and leaving long threads at each end, sew two rows of gathering stitching around the upper edge of the skirt layer between the notches and side seams. Sew the first row 5mm (¼in) in from the edge and the second row 3mm (⅛in) in from the first (see *figure 6*).

STEP 7

Sewing the bodice to the skirt and finishing the skirt

With the bodice right side out, lap the back left placket over the back right placket (as you look at it), matching the centres. Tack the layers together at the bottom edge.

With right sides together, pin the upper edge of the first layer of the skirt to the bottom of the bodice, matching the centres and side seams. Pull up the gathering stitches on the skirt to fit the bodice, making sure the gathers are even (see *figure 7*). Baste and then machine stitch. Press the seam towards the bodice and finish the raw edges. Topstitch on the right side close to the fold of the seam.

Make up the second, third and fourth layers of the skirt in the same way as the first, joining the panels of each layer together to form a circle. Sew gathering stitches around the upper edge of each circle between the notches and side seams (see *step 6*).

Make up the skirt by stitching the upper edge of the second layer to the lower edge of the first, matching the centres and side seams, and pulling up the gathering stitches to fit, as described above. Repeat for the third and fourth layers.

Press the hem allowance on the lower edge of the fourth layer to the wrong side. To form the narrow hem, tuck the raw edge under to meet the crease, and press. Machine stitch the hem in place.

figure 7

STEP 8

Adding the buttons and buttonholes

With the dress right side out, make four vertical buttonholes on the left bodice placket, positioning them 5mm (¼in) from the edge and approximately 4cm (1¾in) apart.

Sew corresponding buttons onto the right bodice placket (see *figure 8*).

figure 8

Silk Chiffon & Lace Dress

This gorgeous party dress epitomizes a true vintage look, with the delicate lace trim being its strong feature. Lace such as this can be readily picked up at vintage fairs and really enhances this type of garment. As you may expect, the original dress on which this pattern is based was a vintage find from Portobello Market some years back and has appeared in my collection in different colours over the last few seasons.

Silk chiffon is really the ideal fabric to use, as the dress has to 'float' when worn. It is a true occasion dress and could even be used as a flower girl's outfit for a wedding.

Materials

Paper for pattern
2.75m (3yd) plain silk chiffon
2.25m (2½yd) matching plain
    cotton for lining
20cm (8in) matching fine netting
    for sleeves
2.6m (3yd) lace trim, 4cm
    (1½in) wide
70cm (28in) piping, 3mm (⅛in)
    diameter
1 hook-and-eye (optional)
Basting thread
Matching sewing threads
Sewing machine and sewing kit
Iron and ironing board

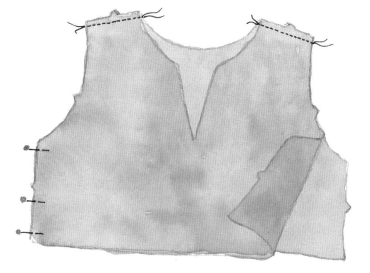

figure 1

STEP 1

Making up the bodice

Starting with the chiffon outer layer, with right sides together, pin and then baste the back of the bodice to the front along the shoulder seams, matching up the notches; machine stitch along the shoulder seams with a 5mm (¼in) seam allowance. Sew along the side seams (see *figure 1*). Press all the seams open and then turn right side out. Repeat for the lining.

Cut a length of lace long enough to fit around the bodice with 1cm (½in) extra for the overlap. Starting 5mm (¼in) beyond one side seam, pin and then baste the trim around the chiffon bodice approximately 2cm (¾in) above the waistline. Turn the other end 5mm (¼in) under, overlapping the first end (see *step 7 overleaf*). Topstitch along both edges of the lace and along the folded edge at the side seam.

With wrong sides together, place the lining inside the chiffon bodice, and baste together around the neckline and armholes, 3mm (⅛in) from the edge.

STEP 2

Constructing the skirt

With right sides together, sew the side seams of the chiffon skirt with a 5mm (¼in) seam allowance. Press the seams to one side and overlock the raw edges.

Using a long stitch on your sewing machine and leaving long threads at both ends, sew one row of gathering stitching around the top edge of the skirt, 5mm (¼in) from the raw edge. Sew a second row of gathering stitching 3mm (⅛in) below the first. Hold the threads tightly on the top of the fabric and gently gather up the material until the top of the skirt is the same width as the waistline of the bodice. Evenly distribute the gathers around the top of the skirt.

Repeat for the lining.

Turn the outer skirt and the lining right sides out. Insert the lining into the skirt, with the right side of the lining to the wrong side of the skirt. Pin and then baste together at the waistline (see *figure 2*).

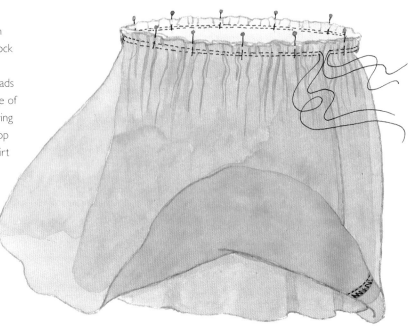

figure 2

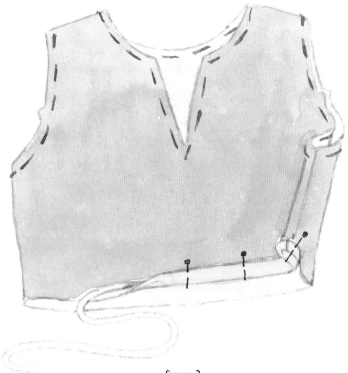

figure 3

STEP 3

Joining the bodice and skirt

Fold and press the bottom edge of the bodice and lining to the wrong side. Starting at one side seam, enclose the piping within the fold and pin and then baste in place (see *figure 3*). Stitch the ends of the piping together and then machine stitch all the way around the bodice as close to the piping as possible.

Press the seam downwards and pin the skirt to the bodice with right sides together. With the bodice facing up, machine stitch along the line you have just sewn, joining the skirt just below the covered piping. Press the seam towards the bodice and overlock the raw edges.

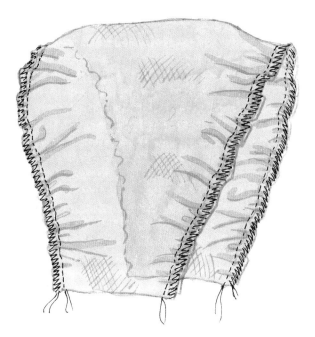

figure 4

STEP 4

Making and attaching the sleeves

Overlock or zigzag stitch the top and bottom edge of the sleeve to prevent the edges from fraying. In the same way as you gathered the skirt (see *step 2*), gather the cap of the sleeves to fit the armholes, allowing for the seam allowance when sewing up the sleeve, and then gather the bottom edge of the sleeves (see *figure 4*).

Cut a 3.2cm- (1¼in-) wide piece of chiffon on the bias, long enough to fit the bottom edge of the sleeve. Fold and press the trim in half with wrong sides together, and press one side of the trim 8mm (⅜in) into the centre fold. Align the raw edge of the trim on the right side with the inside of the bottom edge of the sleeve, and sew with an 8mm (⅜in) seam allowance. Flip the folded side of the trim to the outside of the sleeve and topstitch along the edge.

With right sides together, pin and then baste the front and back of the sleeves together; machine stitch with a 5mm (¼in) seam allowance and overlock the raw edges.

With right sides together, pin and then baste the sleeves into the armholes; machine stitch with 8mm (⅜in) seams and overlock the raw edges.

STEP 5

Completing the neckline

Cut a 2cm- (1in-) wide piece of chiffon on the bias, long enough to fit around the V-shaped neckline with 5mm (¼in) extra at each end. Fold and press each end of the trim 5mm (¼in) to the wrong side. Fold and press the trim in half with wrong sides together, and press one side of the trim 5mm (¼in) into the centre fold. Align the raw edge of the trim on the right side with the inside of the V-neckline and sew with a 5mm (¼in) seam allowance. Flip the folded side of the trim to the outside of the dress and topstitch around the neckline (see *figure 5*).

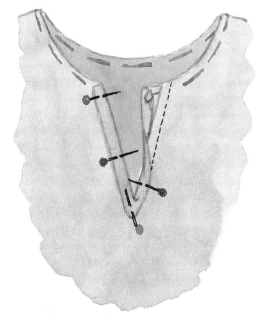

figure 5

STEP 6

Making the collar

Lay the three layers of fabric that make up the collar together, with the lining on the bottom and the two chiffon layers with right sides together on top of it. Sew along the sides and top of the collar with a 5mm (¼in) seam allowance. Clip into the seam allowance along the curves (see figure 6). Turn the chiffon layers right side out, and press.

Cut a 1.5cm- (⅝in-) wide piece of chiffon on the bias, long enough to fit around the neckline of the dress with 5mm (¼in) extra at each end. Fold and press both ends and one long edge of the trim 5mm (¼in) to the wrong side. With the right side of the trim to the top of the collar, align the raw edges and pin and then baste together.

With the right side of the neckline to the right side of the back of the collar, align the raw edges and sew with a 5mm (¼in) seam allowance. Press the seam towards the dress, then flip the folded edge of the trim to the inside of the neckline and topstitch. Topstitch around the outer edge of the collar.

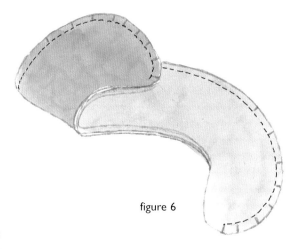

figure 6

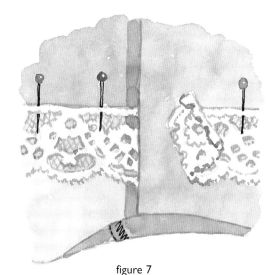

figure 7

STEP 7

Finishing the dress

Cut a length of lace long enough to fit around the skirt approximately 4cm (1½in) from the bottom with 1cm (½in) extra for the overlap. Starting 5mm (¼in) beyond one side seam, pin and then baste the lace around the chiffon skirt. Turn the other end of the lace 5mm (¼in) under, overlapping the first end (see figure 7). Topstitch along both edges of the lace and along the folded end at the side seam.

Serge or use a decorative stitch on the bottom of the chiffon skirt to finish the raw edge. Fold and press the hem of the lining 5mm (¼in) to the wrong side, fold over another 5mm (¼in), press, and then machine stitch along the fold.

If you wish, sew a hook-and-eye to the inside of the neckline.

STEP 8

Decorating the collar

Cut out one of the lace details (for example, a flower) and topstitch it onto the collar where desired.

For the hand-sewn finish on the collar, apply contrasting blanket stitch around the edge, using a double thread (see figure 8). Anchor the knot underneath the collar at the edge. Begin a stitch 5mm (¼in) deep. Pull the needle through the stitch, over the edge of the collar, looping the thread behind the needle point. Make uniform stitches around the collar. Tie a knot in the thread on the underside of the collar to finish.

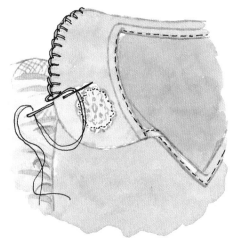

figure 8

Musical Chairs

What You Need – One less chair than the number of children playing the game

What You Do – Arrange the chairs back to back in two rows. When the music is turned on, the players walk or skip around the chairs. When the music stops, the players sit down on the nearest chair. The player left standing is taken out of the game. The remaining players all stand up again and one chair is removed. The music is started again and the game continues. This procedure is repeated until only one person remains. This person is the winner.

Tulip-Shaped Dress

This gorgeous dress with its layered petticoats has a typical 1950s shape that gives it a timeless appeal. It can be styled either in a classic way with soft ballet pumps or in a funkier style with slightly worn canvas boots. The netting underskirt gives it that real occasion feel, which makes it perfect for parties and means it could make an enchanting outfit for a flower girl.

Vintage floral prints work particularly well for this garment, and the shape lends itself to soft poplin or baby cord fabrics.

Materials

Paper for pattern
2.75m (3yd) floral poplin
1.75m (2yd) white netting
1.75m (2yd) white cotton lining
4 buttons, 1cm (⅜in) diameter
Basting thread
Matching sewing thread
Sewing machine and sewing kit
Iron and ironing board

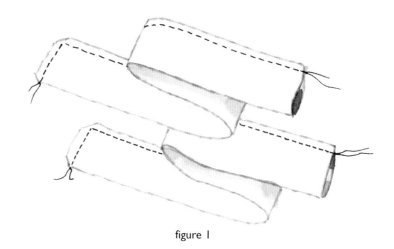

figure 1

STEP 1

Making the sash

Fold each strip for the two sashes in half with right sides together. Sew along the bottom edge and one end with a 5mm (¼in) seam allowance (see *figure 1*).

Clip the corners and press the seams open. Turn the strips right side out and topstitch along the edges of the seams and fold.

STEP 2

Starting the bodice

With right sides together, match the notches for the darts on the front of the bodice and press. Sew the darts on the wrong side of the dress and press towards the centre.

Pin and then baste the unsewn end of one sash to each side of the front bodice, positioning the sashes 1cm (¼in) from the bottom edge on the right side of the bodice (see *figure 2*).

With right sides together and matching the notches on the shoulders, sew the left and right back bodice pieces to the front bodice piece with a 1cm (¼in) seam allowance. Press the seams towards the back bodice and overlock the raw edges.

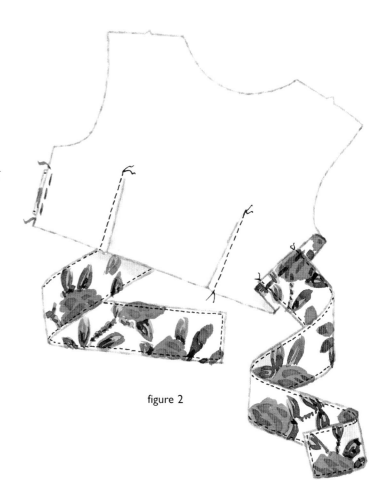

figure 2

STEP 3

Making and attaching the sleeves

Fold and press the bottom edge of the sleeves 5mm (¼in) to the wrong side; fold over and press another 2cm (¾in), and sew the hem in place.

With right sides together, pin and then baste the sleeves to the bodice, matching the notches; machine stitch with a 1cm (½in) seam allowance, and then press the seams towards the sleeves and overlock the raw edges.

With right sides together, pin and then baste each sleeve together from the hem to the armhole; continue down the side seams to the bottom of the bodice, joining the front and back, making sure the sashes are on the inside of the bodice (see *figure 3*). Machine stitch with a 1cm (½in) seam allowance. Press the seams towards the back of the bodice; overlock the raw edges and topstitch the seam allowance at the cuffs.

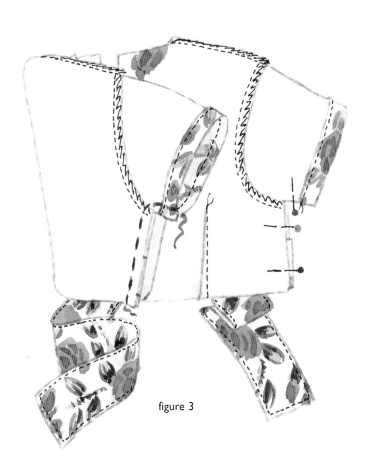

figure 3

figure 4

STEP 4

Gathering and sewing up the skirts

First, cut a vertical slit in the top centre of the back skirt, netting and lining for the button extension, as indicated on the pattern.

Using a long stitch length on the sewing machine and leaving long threads at each end, sew one row of gathering stitching 5mm (¼in) from the edge along the top of the front and back skirt, netting and lining pieces. Sew a second row of gathering stitching 3mm (⅛in) below the first (see *figure 4*). Hold one end of the threads tightly on the top of the fabric and gently gather the material until the top of the skirt pieces match the width of the front and back bodice pieces. Make sure the gathers are evenly distributed.

With right sides together, sew the front and back of the skirt together at the side seams with a 1cm (½in) seam allowance and overlock the raw edges. Repeat for the netting and lining skirts.

figure 5

STEP 5

Attaching the skirts to the bodice

With wrong sides facing out, align the gathered top edges of the three skirts together – place the outer skirt on the inside, the netting in the middle and the lining on the outside. Pin and then baste the skirts together along the top edge.

With right sides together, sew the skirts to the bottom of the bodice. Press the seam towards the bodice; overlock the raw edges and then machine stitch over the seam allowance at the side seams (see *figure 5*).

figure 6

STEP 6

Hemming the skirts

Fold and press the bottom edge of the outer skirt 5mm (¼in) to the wrong side, and then fold over and press another 3cm (1¼in); pin, baste and then machine stitch the hem in place.

Trim the bottom of the netting to the same length – you don't need to hem it.

The lining is 3cm (1¼in) shorter than the outer skirt. Fold and press the bottom edge 5mm (¼in) to the wrong side, and then fold over and press another 1.5cm (⅝in); sew the hem in place (see *figure 6*).

STEP 7

Fitting the button extension

Fold and press one side of the button extension 5mm (¼in) to the wrong side, and then fold and press the folded edge to 5mm (¼in) from the raw edge.

Align the raw edge of the button extension with the inside of the centre back of the dress, with the right side of the extension to the wrong side of the dress; sew with a 5mm (¼in) seam allowance.

Flip the folded edge of the extension to the outside of the centre back of the dress and topstitch in place.

With the dress still inside out, bring the bottom of the left buttonhole extension over the right and stitch them together diagonally from the bottom left corner to 1cm (½in) above the bottom right corner. Press the extension flat, and topstitch a horizontal line straight across the bottom (see *figure 7*).

Make four vertical buttonholes in the centre of the left-hand buttonhole extension, positioning the first one 1cm (½in) from the neckline and spacing the other three evenly 5cm (2in) apart.

Sew four corresponding buttons on the right button extension.

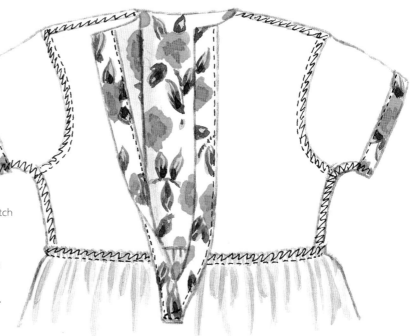

figure 7

figure 8

STEP 8

Finishing the neckline

Cut the seam binding on the bias. Press the ends and one long edge 5mm (¼in) to the wrong side.

With the right side of the binding to the right side of the neckline, pin and then baste the raw edge of the binding to the neckline; machine stitch with a 5mm (¼in) seam allowance.

Fold and press the folded edge of the binding to the inside of the neckline and topstitch along the folded edge and the ends of the binding (see *figure 8*).

Handkerchief-Sleeve Dress

This charming dress has the classic vintage 'handkerchief' sleeve, which has beautiful detailing in the form of the wide broderie lace trimming. The design was based on a dress shape I had as a little girl, and I remember vividly the elegance of the full, wide sleeve. It looks great in soft baby cord, either plain, with an interesting trim such as a rickrack or lace, or printed, as shown here. This style also suits soft voile for summer with pretty trim detailing on the bodice and sleeve edges. Team it with boots and tights for winter and delicate sandals for the summer months.

Materials

Paper for pattern
2.5m (2¾yd) printed baby cord
2.5m (2¾yd) picot-edge trim,
　3mm (⅛in) wide
2.2m (2½yd) broderie lace trim,
　2.5cm (1in) wide
5 buttons, 1cm (⅜in) diameter
Basting thread
Matching sewing threads
Sewing machine and sewing kit
Iron and ironing board

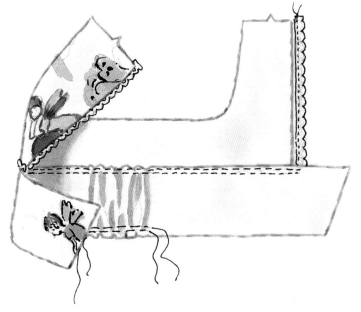

figure 1

STEP 1
Making the bodice

Gather approximately 7cm (2¾in) of the centre of the front bodice piece by sewing two rows of gathering stitching between the markers on the top and bottom edges, the first 5mm (¼in) from the edge and the second 3mm (⅛in) below it.

With right sides together, pin and then machine stitch a length of picot-edge trim onto the seam allowance along the bottom and outer sides of the yoke; then press 5mm (¼in) to the wrong side, so the trim's picot edge becomes the outer edge of the yoke piece.

With right sides together, sew the bodice to the bottom edge of the yoke along the edge of the trim. Press the seam allowance up and topstitch over it (see figure 1).

With right sides together, pin the front yoke to the back bodice at the shoulder seams; machine stitch with a 5mm (¼in) seam allowance and overlock the raw edges.

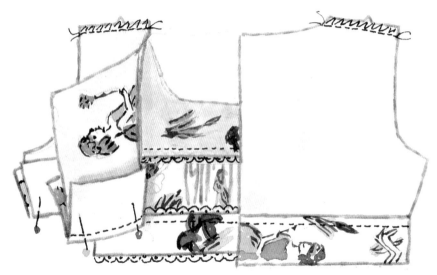

figure 2

STEP 2

Making the waistband and sashes

The waistband is in three sections – one for the front of the dress and two for the back – each made up of an outer and an inner layer.

With right sides together, pin and then machine stitch the picot-edge trim onto the seam allowance along the top of the outer pieces of the waistband; then press 5mm (¼in) to the wrong side, so the picot edge will become the top edge of the waistband.

Align the top edges of the waistband pieces with the bottom edge of the dress bodice pieces, with the right side of the outer waistband to the right side of the bodice and the right side of the inner waistband to the wrong side of the bodice. Sew with a 5mm (¼in) seam allowance. Press the waistband right side out and topstitch 5mm (¼in) below the seam.

With right sides together, pin and then machine stitch the picot-edge trim onto the seam allowance along the bottom double-layered edge of the waistband; then press 5mm (¼in) to the wrong side, so the trim's picot edge becomes the bottom edge of the waistband (see *figure 2*).

Fold each sash in half lengthways with right sides together. Pin and then machine stitch along the bottom edge and one end. Clip the two corners and press the seams open, then turn the tie right side out, and press.

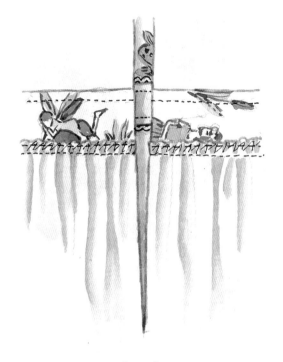

STEP 3

Gathering and attaching the skirts

First, cut a vertical slit in the top centre of the back skirt for the button extension, as indicated on the pattern.

Using a long stitch on your sewing machine, sew two rows of gathering stitching along the top of the front and back skirt pieces: leave long threads at both ends and sew the first row 5mm (¼in) in from the edge and the second row 3mm (⅛in) below the first. Hold the threads tightly on the top of the fabric and gently gather the material until each piece is the same width as the bottom of the corresponding bodice pieces. Evenly distribute the gathers along the skirts.

With right sides together, sew the top of the skirts to the bottom of the waistband along the edge of the trim. Press the seam allowance up, overlock the raw edges and topstitch along the edge (see *figure 3*).

figure 3

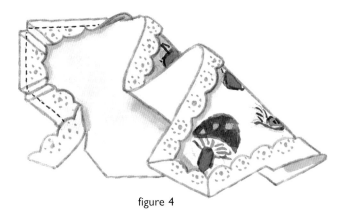

figure 4

STEP 4

Trimming and attaching the sleeves

Clip 5mm (¼in) into both sides of the sleeve at the point where it will meet the side seams of the bodice under the armhole.

With wrong sides together, sew the broderie lace trim around the sleeve between the two points. At the corners, sew the lace together on the diagonal so that it lies flat. Flip the lace to the right side of the sleeve (see *figure 4*). Clip the lace to match the points on the sleeve and baste together. Topstitch along both edges of the lace.

Gather the top of the sleeve in the same way as the skirts (see *step 3*). With right sides together, sew the sleeves into the armholes; press the seam allowance towards the bodice, overlock the raw edges and topstitch along the edge.

STEP 5

Sewing up the dress

With the seam at the bottom, baste the open end of each sash to either end of the front waistband on the right side.

With right sides together and making sure the loose ends of the sashes are on the inside, pin and then baste the front and back of the dress together at the side seams (see *figure 5*). Starting at the armhole and working down the bodice to the bottom of the skirt, machine stitch with a 1cm (½in) seam allowance.

Fold and press the bottom edge of the skirt 5mm (¼in) to the wrong side, and then fold over and press another 2cm (¾in); machine stitch along the edge of the hem.

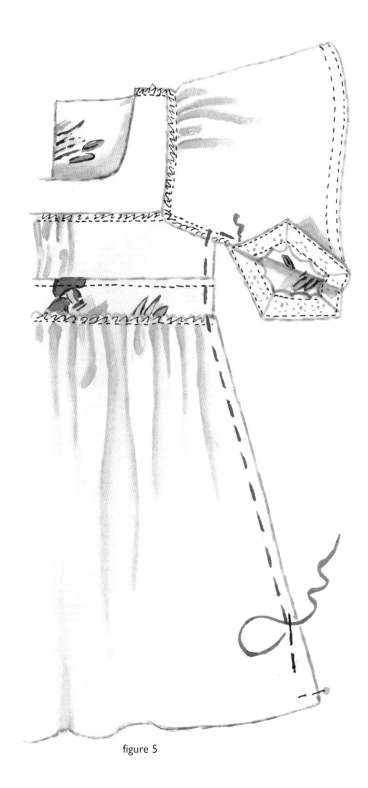

figure 5

figure 6

STEP 6

Attaching the button extension

With wrong sides together, fold and press the button extension lengthways into thirds, but leave one edge 5mm (¼in) longer than the other (see *figure 6*).

Align the raw edge of the button extension with the inside of the centre back of the dress, with the right side of the extension to the wrong side of the dress; sew with a 5mm (¼in) seam. Flip the folded edge of the extension to the outside of the dress and topstitch.

Fold the left side of the extension back on itself to the wrong side of the dress, and tack in place to hold. Bring the left buttonhole extension over the top of the right button extension and topstitch straight across the base of the extension, joining both sides together.

Make five vertical buttonholes in the left side of the extension, positioning the first one centrally approximately 2cm (¾in) from the edge of the neckline and spacing four more 4cm (1½in) apart. Sew five corresponding buttons onto the right side of the extension.

STEP 7

Finishing the neckline

With right sides together, pin and then machine stitch a length of picot-edge trim onto the seam allowance around the neckline of the dress; then press 5mm (¼in) to the wrong side, so the picot edge is at the top.

Cut the seam binding on the bias and fold and press both long edges and the ends 5mm (¼in) to the wrong side. Beginning at the centre back, align the top folded edge of the binding with the edge of the fold of the seam allowance, next to the picot edge, easing the binding around the corners; pin and then baste in place (see *figure 7*). Topstitch along both edges and ends of the binding.

figure 7

Butterfly Cakes

This butterfly cake recipe or fairy cake recipe is quick and easy to make and great for children's parties.

110g (4oz) soft margarine
110g (4oz) caster sugar
2 eggs
110g (4oz) self-raising flour
1 tsp baking powder

1 Pre-heat the oven to 200°C/400°F/gas mark 6.
2 Get about 18 paper cases ready.
3 Measure all the ingredients into a large bowl and beat well for 2–3 minutes until the mixture is well blended.
4 Half-fill the paper cases with mixture.
5 Bake for about 15–20 minutes until the cakes are well risen and golden brown. Allow to cool.

For the icing:
175g (6oz) butter
350g (12oz) icing sugar, sifted
Raspberry coulis or jam

1 Beat the butter until it is soft, add the icing sugar gradually and mix together until smooth.
2 Cut a slice from the top of each cake and cut the slice in half.
3 Pipe a swirl of icing into the centre of each cake and place the half slices into it like butterfly wings.
4 Using a teaspoon, drizzle a little raspberry coulis or jam over the top of the icing.

1950s Pin-Tuck Dress

The silhouette for this dress came from a children's vintage dress from the 1950s and has classic pin-tucking on the front bodice. The large buttons are a prominent feature on the front of the dress, so here we have used covered buttons so as not to detract from the busy Spanish Dancing Girls print, but if you choose a plain fabric, more interesting decorative buttons could be used to provide additional embellishment.

This dress is so pretty when styled as an occasion piece for parties, but it looks equally good dressed down with ankle socks, canvas boots and a baseball hat.

Materials

Paper for pattern

2.25m (2.5yd) printed cotton poplin

80cm (31½in) picot-edge trim, 7mm (¼in) wide

3 covered buttons, 2cm (¾in) diameter

35cm (13¾in) elastic, 5cm (2in) wide

40 x 5cm (15¾ x 2in) iron-on interfacing for collar

Basting thread

Matching sewing threads

Sewing machine and sewing kit

Iron and ironing board

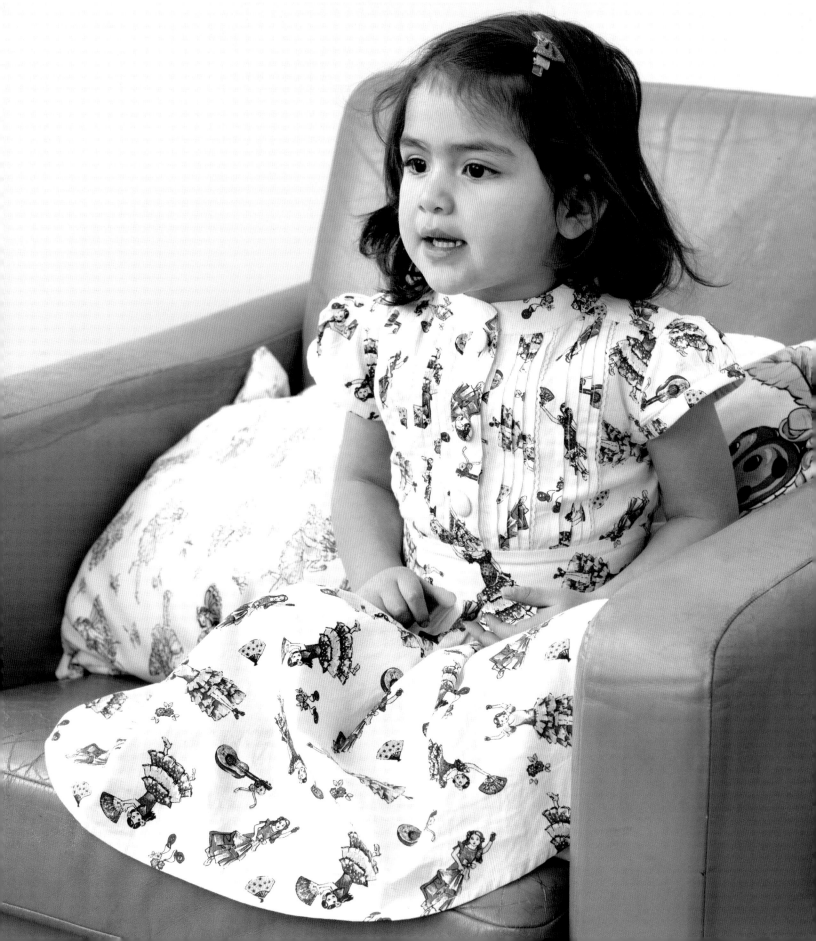

figure 1

STEP 1

Making the pin-tucks

Both sides of the front bodice panel feature two sets of four 5mm- (¼in-) wide pin-tucks with 2cm (¾in) between the sets.

With wrong sides together, fold and press the bodice panels on the straight grain at the notches for the pin-tucks, using pins as markers; machine-stitch 5mm (¼in) in from each fold to form the pin-tucks.

Lay the bodice panels flat, with right sides up, and press the pin-tucks towards the side seams.

Cut four lengths of trim to the same length as the outer pin-tuck in each set of four. Pin the trim in place under the fourth pin-tuck in each set, so that the raw edge is hidden under the fold of the pin-tuck and the picot edge is visible. Topstitch each strip of trim in place (see *figure 1*).

Baste the pleats down along the top and bottom edges of both bodice panels.

figure 2

STEP 2

Gathering the back bodice

Choose a long stitch length on your sewing machine and leaving long threads at both ends, sew one row of gathering stitching 5mm (¼in) in along the centre top of the back bodice between the markers. Sew a second row 3mm (⅛in) below the first. Hold the threads tightly on the right side of the fabric and gently gather up the material to fit the width of the back yoke. Distribute the gathers even along the centre of the bodice, leaving equal portions ungathered at the sides (see *figure 2*).

figure 3

STEP 3

Making and attaching the yoke

Align the top of the yoke lining with the top of the front bodice, with the right side of the yoke lining to the wrong side of the front bodice; pin and baste along both seams. With right sides together, pin and then baste the top of the yoke to the top of the front bodice; machine stitch along both seams with a 5mm (¼in) seam allowance. Press the yoke and lining to the back, so that wrong sides are together, and topstitch over the fold.

Press the bottom edges of the yoke and the lining 5mm (¼in) to the wrong side. Push the seam allowance at the top of the back bodice into the bottom of the yoke, sandwiching it between the two pieces; pin, baste and then topstitch along the edge (see figure 3).

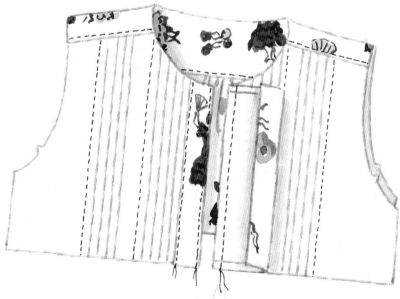

figure 4

STEP 4

Making the button and buttonhole extensions

Fold and press both ends of the button and buttonhole extensions 5mm (¼in) to the wrong side. Press the strips lengthways into thirds but leave one edge 5mm (¼in) longer than the other.

Align the raw edge of each extension with the inside of the centre front, with the right side of the extension to the wrong side of the bodice; sew with a 5mm (¼in) seam allowance. Flip the folded side of the extension to the right side of the dress and topstitch down both sides (see figure 4).

Make three vertical buttonholes centrally in the left extension (as you look at it), positioning the first one 5mm (¼in) from the top and spacing the other two 4cm (1½in) apart beneath it. Sew three corresponding buttons onto the right extension. We used self-covering buttons, which come with easy-to-follow instructions.

STEP 5

Creating the collar

Apply iron-on interfacing to the wrong side of the collar front, following the manufacturer's instructions. With right sides together, sew the front and back pieces of the collar together along the sides and top with a 5mm (¼in) seam allowance (see *figure 5*). Clip into the seam allowance at the curves, turn the collar right side out and press, then press the bottom edge of the back of the collar 5mm (¼in) to the wrong side.

Align the bottom edge of the front of the collar to the neckline, with the right side of the collar front to the inside of the bodice. Flip the folded edge of the back of the collar over the seam allowance and pin and then baste it to the right side of the neckline. Topstitch along the folded edge, and then continue topstitching all the way around the edge of the collar.

figure 5

STEP 6

Assembling the waistband and sashes

The back of the waistband is elasticated and the front is not.

Attach the front (non-elasticated) waistband to the front bodice first. Do up the buttons and tack the bottom of the button extensions together. With right sides together, align the top edge of the waistband with the bottom edge of the bodice; pin and then baste in place (see *figure 6*). Pin and then baste the top edge of the waistband lining to the bottom edge of the bodice, with the right side of the lining to the wrong side of the bodice. Machine stitch all three layers together with a 5mm (¼in) seam allowance. Press the waistband down so the wrong sides are together.

Attach the top edge of the back waistband and lining to the back bodice in the same way. Insert the strip of elastic between the back waistband and lining; tack both ends to the ends of the waistband lining, pulling it tight to match the length.

With right sides together, fold each sash in half lengthways. Pin and then baste along one end and the bottom edge; machine stitch with a 5mm (¼in) seam allowance. Clip the corners and turn the sashes right sides out and press.

Turn the bodice wrong side out and tack one sash to each end of the front waistband, aligning the open end of the sash to the waistband lining with the top of the sash flush with the top of the waistband, so that the sash is clear of the seam allowance at the bottom of the waistband.

figure 6

figure 7

STEP 7

Making and attaching the skirt

Following the method described for gathering the back bodice (see *step 2*), sew two rows of gathering stitching along the top of the front and back skirts, 5mm (¼in) and 8mm (⅜in) in from the edge. Gather the top of both skirts until they fit the waistbands (see *figure 7*).

Join the front skirt to the front waistband, aligning the top edge of the skirt to the bottom edge of the waistband with the right side of the skirt to the right side of the waistband. Sew with an 8mm (⅜in) seam allowance. Press the seam up and overlock the raw edges.

Join the back skirt to the back of the waistband in the same way.

STEP 8

Sewing up the side seams

With right sides together, pin and then baste the front and back of the dress together along the side seams, making sure the sashes are inside the dress and clear of the seams (see *figure 8*). Starting at the armholes at the top of the bodice and working down the dress to the bottom of the skirt, machine stitch with a 1cm (½in) seam allowance.

Fold and press the bottom edge of the skirt 5mm (¼in) to the wrong side, then fold over and press an additional 5mm (¼in); pin, baste and then machine stitch the hem.

figure 8

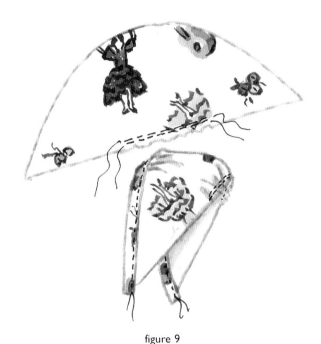

figure 9

STEP 9

Making and attaching the sleeves

In the same way as for the back bodice (see *step 2*), sew two rows of gathering stitching along the top and bottom edges of each sleeve between the markers. Gather the centre bottom of each sleeve until it fits the trim, and gather the cap of each sleeve until it fits into the armhole between the notches on the bodice.

With right sides together, fold and press both strips for the trim in half on the cross grain. Open out each strip and then fold and press one long edge 8mm (⅜in) into the centre fold.

Align the raw edge of the trim with the bottom edge of the sleeve, with the right side of the trim to the wrong side of the sleeve; sew with an 8mm (⅜in) seam allowance. Flip the folded side of the trim to the right side of the sleeve and topstitch along the fold (see *figure 9*).

With right sides together, fit the sleeves into the armholes; sew with an 8mm (⅜in) seam allowance. Press the seams to the inside and overlock the raw edges.

Fold and press the edges of each seam binding 5mm (¼in) to the wrong side. Press the seam allowance at the bottom of the armholes to the inside of the dress. Pin and then baste the bindings onto the bottom inside edge of the armholes, evenly overlapping the edges of the sleeves. Topstitch all the way around the edge of the seam bindings.

Pass the Parcel

This is a traditional party favourite with children of all ages, and you can be as extravagant as you wish in terms of the final prize. Wrap the main present – it could just be a bar of chocolate or packet of sweets – in several layers of paper (one for each child attending the party). You can use newspaper, brown paper or inexpensive wrapping paper – a different colour for each layer, perhaps – and secure it with sticky tape. If you wish, enlose a small treat within every layer, so that each child gets something. The players sit in a circle and one of them holds the parcel. When the music starts, the parcel is passed clockwise around the circle from child to child. Each time the music is stopped, the child holding the parcel removes one layer of wrapping. The music is then restarted and the parcel passed around again. The adult controlling the music should try to ensure that every child has a turn at unwrapping the parcel. The game continues until someone removes the last layer of wrapping and so wins the prize.

Boy's Pin-Tuck Shirt

This boy's formal yet fun shirt is a classic shirt shape scaled down to a pint-sized version. The pin-tucks are a great vintage look, which translates really well on this garment, especially when teamed up with interesting buttons. The buttons used here were found in an amazing trims shop called Temptation Alley on Portobello Road. There are lots of similar specialist button shops, and scouring markets and websites for vintage buttons can turn up some great treasures that can transform garments such as this.

Good-grade cotton poplin is the obvious choice for this shirt, but why not look at other more quirky options such as yarn-dyed stripes or even gingham checks.

Materials

Paper for pattern
1.70m (2yd) cotton poplin
8 buttons, 13mm (½in) diameter
Basting thread
Matching sewing thread
Sewing machine and sewing kit
Iron and ironing board

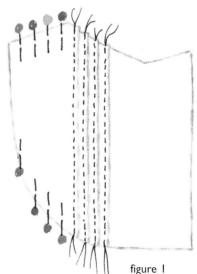

figure 1

STEP 1
Making the pin-tucks

Fold and press the bodice panel on the straight grain at the notch for the first pin-tuck. Topstitch straight down the edge of the fold. Flatten the material and press the pleat towards the centre front. Repeat for each pin-tuck on both bodice panels (see *figure 1*).

STEP 2
Sewing up the bodice

With right sides together, sew the pin-tuck panels into the right and left front bodices. Press the seams away from the pin-tuck panels, overlock the raw edges and topstitch around the curve of the panel, catching the edge of the seam allowance.

Hem or overlock the edge of the button plackets, and then fold and press the plackets to the inside of the shirt along the fold line. Machine stitch the seam allowance of the button plackets to the bodice, from the bottom of the pin-tuck panel up to the neckline.

With right sides together, align the notches at the shoulders and sew the left and right front bodice pieces to the back bodice (see figure 2). Press the seams towards the back and then overlock the raw edges.

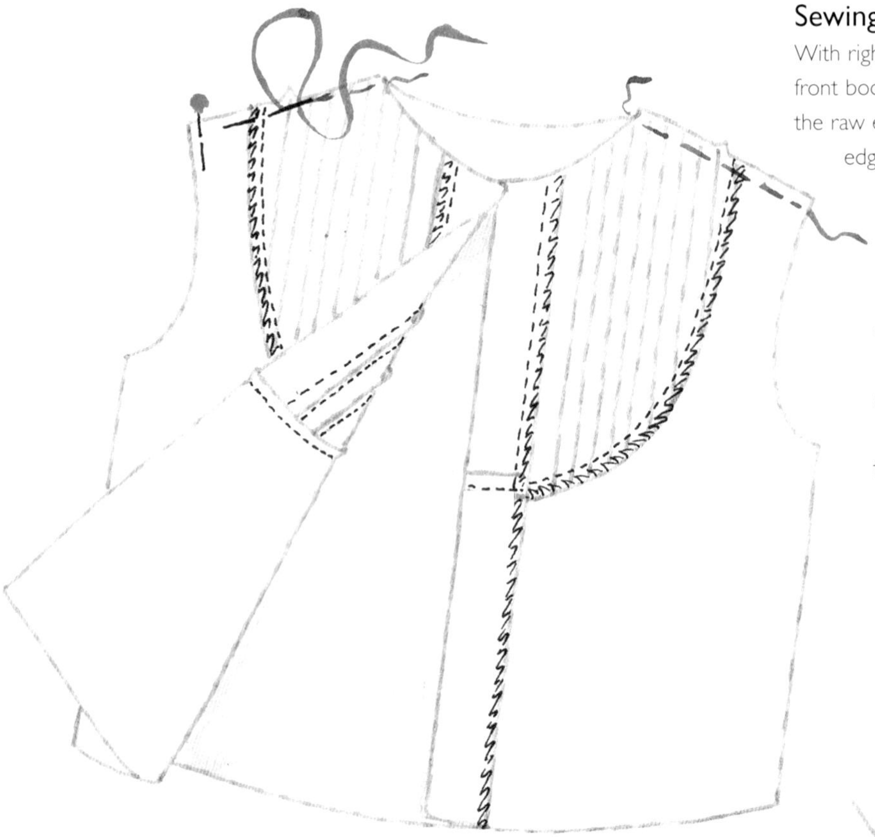

figure 2

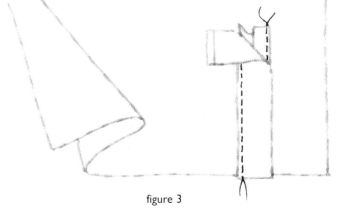

figure 3

STEP 3
Making the cuff laps

Fold and press the narrow lap into thirds, but leave one edge 5mm (¼in) longer than the other. Align the raw edge of the lap with the wrong side of the lower side of the sleeve; sew with a 5mm (¼in) seam allowance. Flip the folded side of the lap to the right side of the sleeve and topstitch along the edge.

Fold and press the larger lap into thirds, but leave one edge 5mm (¼in) longer than the other. Fold and press the top (non-cuff) end of the lap 5mm (¼in) to the wrong side. Align the raw edge of the lap with the wrong side of the top of the sleeve, with the folded end away from the cuff; sew with a 5mm (¼in) seam allowance.

The large lap extends beyond the cuff opening on the right side of the shirt, so clip the top corner of the seam allowance diagonally and clip the corner off the underside of the top of the lap (see figure 3). Flip the folded side of the lap to the right side of the sleeve and topstitch along the edge. Topstitch a square around the overlapping extension to secure.

STEP 4

Attaching the sleeves and sewing up the side seams

Using a long stitch on your sewing machine, sew a row of gathering stitching 5mm (¼in) in along the curved cap of the sleeves and gather to fit the armholes. With right sides together, match up the notches on the sleeves and the bodice, and pin and baste the sleeves in place; machine stitch with a 5mm (¼in) seam allowance, sewing over the gathering stitching. Press the seam allowance towards the bodice, overlock the raw edges and then topstitch over the edge of the seam allowance.

Starting at the bottom of each sleeve, with right sides together, pin and then baste along the length of the sleeves. Continue from the armholes down the side seams of the shirt, joining the front and back bodices together (see figure 4). Machine stitch with a 1cm (½in) seam allowance. Press the seams to one side and overlock the raw edges.

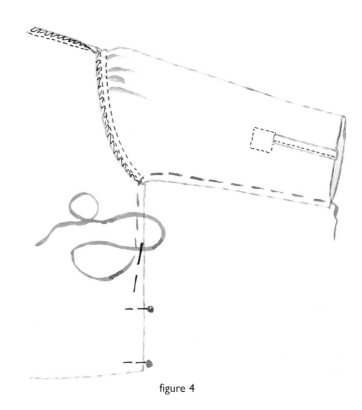

figure 4

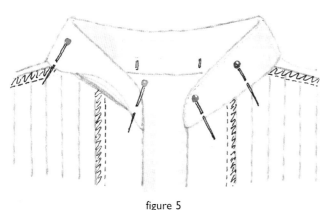

figure 5

STEP 5

Making and attaching the collar

With right sides together, sew the front and back pieces of the collar together along the sides and top edge with a 5mm (¼in) seam allowance. Clip into the seam allowance along the curves, turn the collar right side out, and press. Press the front edge of the collar 5mm (¼in) the wrong side.

With right sides together, sew the back of the collar to the bodice with a 5mm (¼in) seam allowance. Flip the folded edge of the front of the collar over the seam allowance at the neckline and topstitch to the inside of the shirt (see figure 5). Continue the topstitching all the way around the outer edge of the collar.

STEP 6

Finishing the cuffs

Match the notches to make two tucks in the bottom edge of the sleeves, and tack. Then gather the bottom of each sleeve to fit the width of the cuff.

Fold and press both ends of each cuff 5mm (¼in) to the wrong side. Press the cuffs in half lengthways, and press one edge 5mm (¼in) to the wrong side. Align the raw edge of each cuff to the bottom of the sleeve, with the right side of the cuff to the wrong side of the sleeve (see figure 6); sew with a 5mm (¼in) seam allowance. Flip the folded side of the cuff to the right side of the sleeve and topstitch around the edge of the cuff.

Make a horizontal buttonhole in each cuff, centrally below the wider lap and 5mm (¼in) in. Sew a corresponding button below the narrower lap.

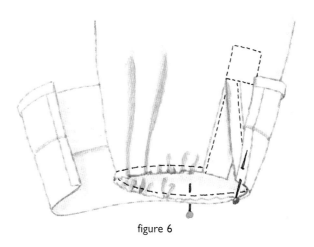

figure 6

figure 7

Hide and Seek

The object of Hide and Seek is for the child who is 'it' to find the other players who are hiding. First of all, choose who is going to be 'it'. That person closes or covers their eyes and counts to 50. While he or she is counting, the other players run away and find places to hide. The person who is 'it' then goes looking for the other players. When he finds one, they are out of the game. The last player to be found wins and becomes the new 'it'.

STEP 7
Finishing the shirt

Fold and press the bottom edge of the shirt 5mm (¼in) to the wrong side. Turn the hem up an additional 5mm (¼in) and machine stitch.

Make a horizontal buttonhole in the centre of the right side of the collar, 5mm (¼in) from the edge. Make five vertical buttonholes in the right buttonhole placket, positioning the first one 3cm (1¼in) below the collar in the centre of the placket and spacing the other four below it, approximately 4cm (1½in) apart. Sew corresponding buttons onto the left side of the collar and button placket.

Bedtime

Children's bedrooms should be retreats of fantasy, full of toys, books and pictures to fuel the imagination. Sweet dreams are guaranteed with these lovely projects inspired by old-fashioned sleepovers. Choose vintage prints for the duvet set and pyjamas to take your child safely to the land of nod.

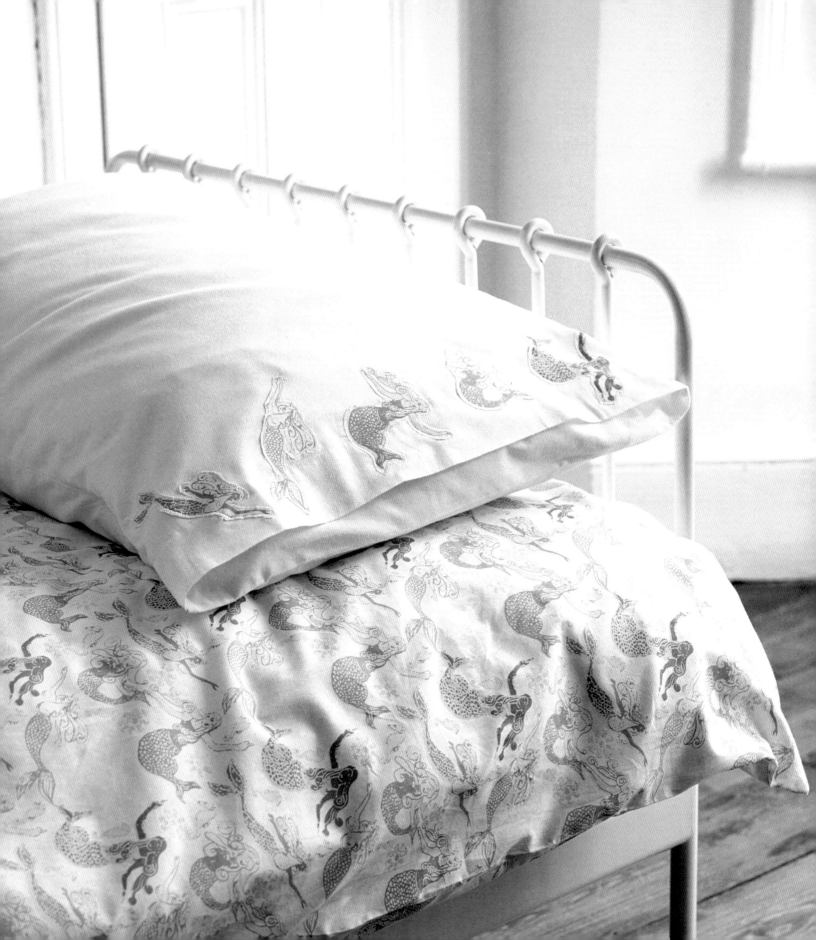

Duvet Set

To give your child's room an individual touch, make their bedding in unusual vintage prints. You can often source good-quality vintage sheets that can be cut up and sewn together to make a duvet cover or pillowcases. Damaged areas can be cut away or covered with appliqué. This duvet is made in a pretty Mermaid print, with the edge of a plain white pillowcase decorated with appliqué shapes cut out from the main pattern. Vintage florals – for girls – or conversational prints such as this are an ideal choice and can be matched with a laundry or toy bag (see page 132) and a notice board (see page 70) for a coordinated look.

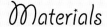

Materials

4.3m (4¾yd) printed cotton for
    single duvet
1.1m (1¼yd) printed or plain
    cotton for a standard pillowcase
For appliqué (optional): iron-on
    fabric adhesive and contrasting
    thread
3 buttons, 2cm (¾in) diameter
Basting thread
Machine thread
Sewing machine and sewing kit
Iron and ironing board

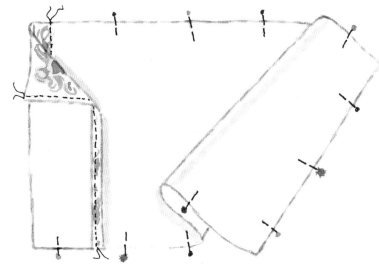

figure 1

STEP 1

Making the pillowcase

Cut one rectangle of fabric measuring 52 × 85.5cm (20½ × 33½in); cut another rectangle measuring 52 × 96.5cm (20½ × 38in).

    Fold and press one end of the shorter rectangle 4.5cm (1¾in) to the wrong side, and then fold over and press another 5cm (2in); sew along the edge to hem.

    Fold and press one end of the longer rectangle 5mm (¼in) to the wrong side, and then fold over and press another 1cm (½in); sew along the edge to hem.

    Lay the longer rectangle right side up on your work surface. With right sides together, lay the shorter rectangle on top, aligning the three raw edges. Fold the hemmed edge of the longer rectangle over the hemmed edge of the shorter rectangle, so the right side of the overlap is to the wrong side of the shorter rectangle, and line up the side seams. Sew around the sides and bottom with a 1cm (½in) seam allowance (see figure 1). Overlock the raw edges, and then turn the pillowcase right side out and press.

    If you have made a plain pillowcase (or to customize a bought one), cut out appropriate shapes from scraps of your main fabric and follow the appliqué instructions on page 132 to decorate the hemmed edge.

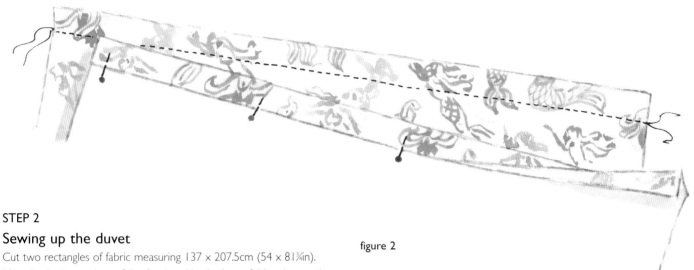

STEP 2

Sewing up the duvet

Cut two rectangles of fabric measuring 137 × 207.5cm (54 × 81¾in). Hem the bottom edges of the front and back pieces: fold and press the bottom end of each piece 5mm (¼in) to the wrong side, and then fold over and press another 3cm (1¼in); sew along the edge (see *figure 2*).

  With right sides together, sew the front and back of the duvet cover together along the top and sides with a 1cm (½in) seam allowance, and overlock the raw edges.

figure 2

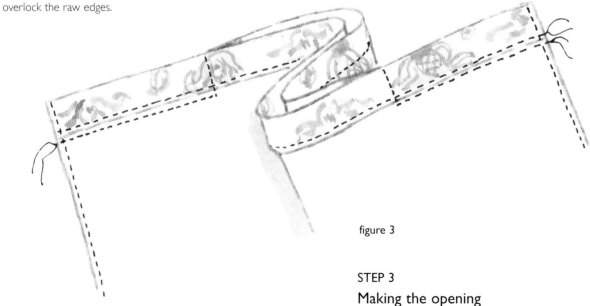

figure 3

STEP 3

Making the opening

To create an opening in the bottom centre of the duvet cover, pin the hemmed edges together, but machine stitch only 30cm (12in) in from the side seams, with a 4cm (1½in) seam allowance. At the end of each 30cm- (12in-) line of stitching, sew at right angles up to the edge of the hems (see *figure 3*). Turn the duvet right side out and press.

STEP 4

Adding the buttons and buttonholes

Make three horizontal buttonholes centrally in the turned-in hem of the opening on the front of the cover, positioning them 15cm (6in) apart.

Sew corresponding buttons on the turned-in hem of the opening on the back of the duvet cover (see figure 4).

figure 4

Classic Boy's Pyjamas

Made up from an original vintage pattern, these lovely pyjamas conjure up nostalgic images of fireside cocoa and bedtime stories. They are a timeless shape and are best made in cotton poplin, either in prints, gingham checks or stripes. For colder months choose brushed cotton to give a cosier feel. You could trim the cuffs, collar and pocket with contrasting trim or, for a personal touch, embroider the child's initials on the pocket.

Twinkle, twinkle, little star,
How I wonder what you are!
Up above the world so high,
Like a diamond in the sky!

Repeat: *Twinkle, twinkle, little star,
How I wonder what you are!*

When the blazing sun is gone,
When he nothing shines upon,
Then you show your little light,
Twinkle, twinkle, all the night.
(*repeat)

Then the traveller in the dark,
Thanks you for your tiny spark,
He could not see which way to go,
If you did not twinkle so.
(*repeat)

In the dark blue sky you keep,
And often through my curtains peep,
For you never shut your eye,
Till the sun is in the sky.
(*repeat)

As your bright and tiny spark,
Lights the traveller in the dark,
Though I know not what you are,
Twinkle, twinkle, little star.
(*repeat)

Materials

Paper for pattern
3.7m (4yd) gingham cotton poplin
4 buttons, 1cm (⅜in) diameter
Basting thread
Matching sewing thread
Sewing machine and sewing kit
Iron and ironing board
Safety pin

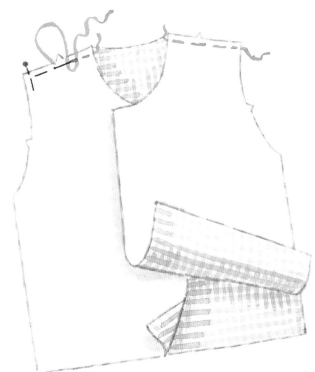

figure 1

STEP 1

Starting the bodice

With right sides together, align the notches at the shoulders and sew the front and back bodice pieces together with a 5mm (¼in) seam allowance, (see *figure 1*). Press the seams to the back and overlock the raw edges.

STEP 2

Adding the sleeves

Fold and press the bottom edge of the sleeve 5mm (¼in) to the wrong side, and then fold over and press another 2cm (¾in); machine stitch the hem in place.

With right sides together, pin the cap of each sleeve to the bodice; baste and then machine stitch with a 5mm (¼in) seam allowance. Press the seam allowance towards the bodice and overlock the raw edges.

Beginning at the cuffs, pin and then baste the front and back of each sleeve together. At the armholes, continue pinning down the side seams, joining the front and back bodice pieces together (see *figure 2*). Machine stitch with a 5mm (¼in) seam allowance, and then overlock the raw edges.

figure 2

STEP 3

Creating the collar

With right sides together, pin the front and back of the collar together. Baste and then machine stitch along the sides and top of the collar with a 5mm (¼in) seam allowance.

Clip the corners, press the seam open and then turn the collar right side out and press. Fold and press the raw edge on the front of the collar 5mm (¼in) to the wrong side. With right sides together, sew the back of the collar onto the back of the bodice neckline with a 5mm (¼in) seam allowance. Press the seam allowance inside the collar.

Fold and press the centre edges of the front bodice 5mm (¼in) to the wrong side, and then fold over another 5mm (¼in); sew the hems. Fold over another 3.5cm (1⅛in) on each side, and press to form the button and buttonhole plackets.

Tuck the seam allowance of the top of the plackets 5mm (¼in) to the inside, clipping into the material so that the portion overlapping the end of the collar lies flat within it, and press.

Bring the folded edge of the collar over the top of the seam allowance and pin in place (see *figure 3*). Topstitch the front of the collar to the inside of the shirt, and then continue topstitching all the way along the outer edge of the plackets.

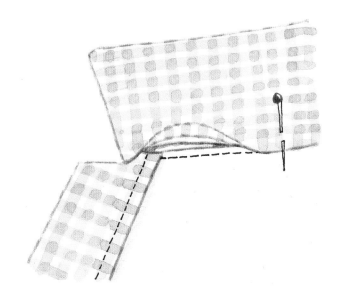

figure 3

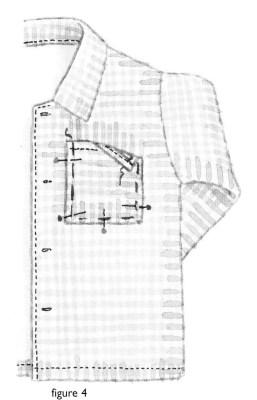

figure 4

STEP 4

Finishing the shirt

Fold and press the bottom edge of the shirt 5mm (¼in) to the wrong side, and then fold over and press another 2cm (¾in); machine stitch around the hem of the bodice.

Make four horizontal buttonholes in the right-hand placket, positioning the first 1cm (½in) from the top and edge of the placket and spacing the other three 9cm (3½in) apart.

Fold and press the top edge of the pocket 5mm (¼in) to the wrong side, and then fold over and press another 2cm (¾in); machine stitch in place. Fold and press the sides and bottom of the pocket 1cm (½in) to the wrong side, and pin and baste. Pin the pocket onto the front bodice, approximately halfway between the top two buttonholes and halfway between the armhole and the placket (see *figure 4*); topstitch around the sides and bottom edge to secure the pocket to the bodice.

STEP 5

Starting the bottoms

With right sides together, match up the front and back pieces. Sew along the side seams with a 1cm (½in) seam allowance. Press the seams to one side and overlock the raw edges.

Fold and press the bottom edge of each leg 5mm (¼in) to the wrong side, and then fold over another 2cm (¾in) and pin in place (see *figure 5*); machine stitch the hems in place.

figure 5

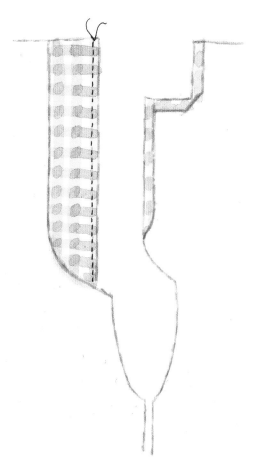

figure 6

STEP 6

Making the fly front

On the front of the left leg, fold the edge of the fly extension 1cm (½in) to the wrong side. Fold and press the extension on the straight grain so the seam allowance is 5mm (¼in) at the curve of the crotch. Fold over and press another 4cm (1½in); pin the fly extension in place and then topstitch along the edge, stopping when you reach the curve.

On the front of the right leg, make a diagonal 5mm (¼in) clip between the fly extension and the waistband. Fold over and press the 5mm (¼in) seam allowance on the waistband and top of the fly extension. Fold and press the edge of the fly extension 1cm (½in) to the wrong side, again folding the extension on the straight grain so that the seam allowance is 5mm (¼in) at the curve of the crotch. Fold over and press another 2.5cm (1in) (see *figure 6*); pin and then machine stitch the fly extension.

With right sides together and a 5mm (¼in) seam allowance, sew the left and right front pieces together, from the bottom of the crotch past the curving portion of the fly extension. At that point, secure the right extension over the left by topstitching horizontally across both extensions to meet the topstitching on the left side.

STEP 7

Finishing the bottoms

Sew the back together from the waistband to the bottom of the crotch. Press the seam to one side and overlock the raw edges.

With right sides together, join the front and back of each leg together. Working from the hem of the right leg up to the crotch and then down to the hem of the left leg, sew with a 5mm (¼in) seam allowance (see figure 7). Press the seam to one side and overlock the raw edges.

Fold and press the edge of the waistband 5mm (¼in) to the wrong side, and then fold over and press another 2cm (¾in). At the centre front of the waistband, make two vertical buttonholes for the drawstring approximately 3cm (1¼in) apart. Machine stitch along the edge of the waistband to create a channel for the drawstring.

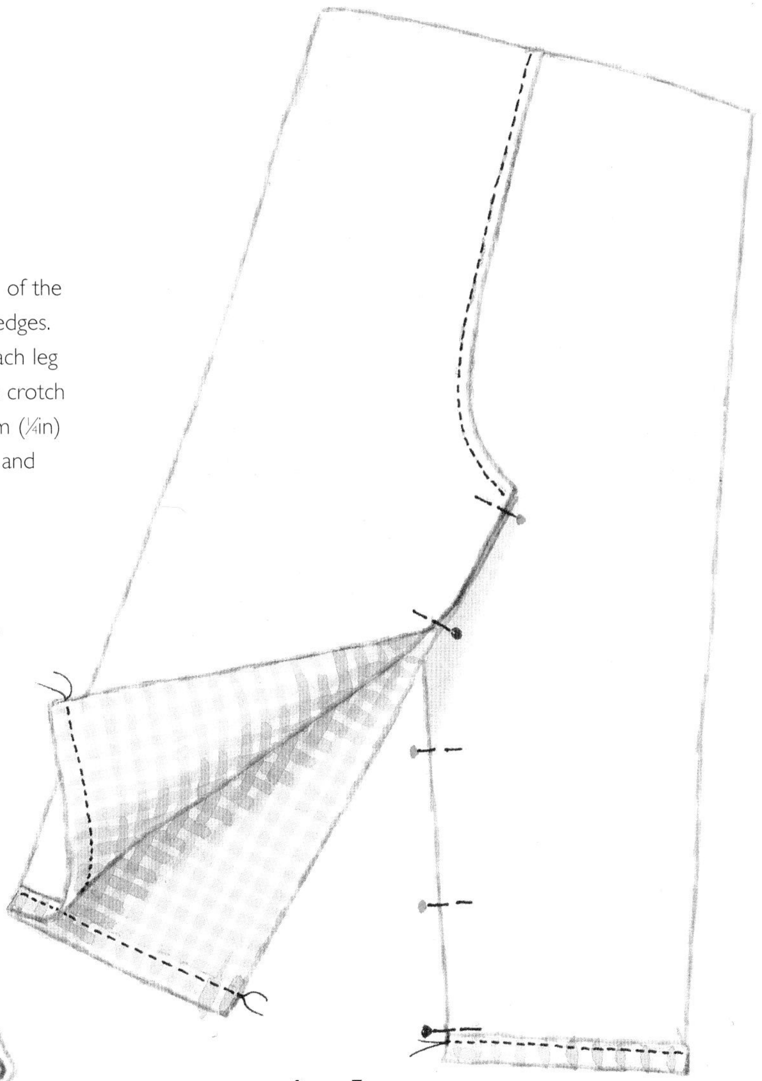

figure 7

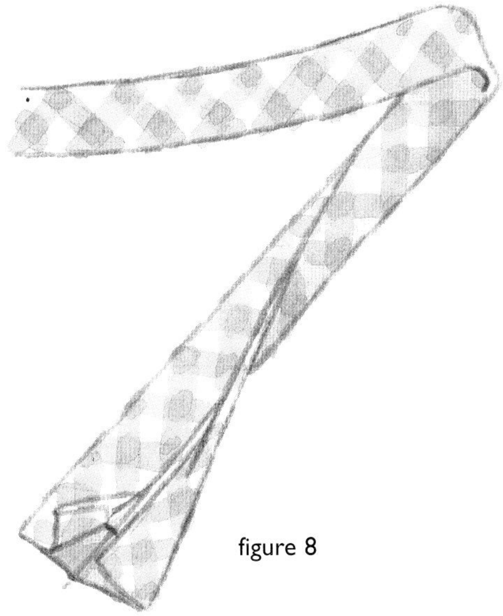

figure 8

STEP 8

Making the drawstring

Make sure the drawstring is cut out on the cross grain. Fold and press the ends of the strip 1cm (½in) to the wrong side. Fold and press the strip in half on the cross grain, with wrong sides together. Open it out, then press both raw edges into the centre fold, and fold and press the strip in half again, so that it is in four layers (see figure 8). Topstitch all the way around the edge.

Using a safety pin, thread the drawstring through the waistband.

Girl's Summer Pyjamas

As is the case for lots of my collection, the inspiration for this garment came from a vintage clothes pattern. The A-line shape of the top and the trousers gathered in at the ankles give the pyjamas a real nostalgic feel.

Dressing up in pretty nightwear is a little girl's dream, so vintage-inspired floral prints on cotton poplin or soft voile lend themselves perfectly to these lightweight summer pyjamas. Plain fabrics in delicate pastels can be trimmed with lengths of vintage lace or decorative ribbon to add that all-important attention to detail.

Materials

Paper for pattern
3.7m (4yd) printed cotton voile
3.7m (4yd) plain cotton lining
140cm (55in) double-folded bias
  binding (or you can make your
  own from the lining fabric by
  cutting strips on the bias)
4 buttons, 12mm (½in) diameter
50cm (19½in) elastic, 1cm- (⅜in-)
  wide (for the waistband)
Two 20cm (8in) lengths elastic,
  5mm- (¼in-) wide (for the ankles)
Basting thread
Matching sewing thread
Sewing machine and sewing kit
Iron and ironing board
Safety pin

figure 1

STEP 1

Joining the front bodice and yoke

Choose a long stitch on the sewing machine and, leaving long threads at both ends, sew one row of gathering stitching along the top of the front bodice pieces, 5mm (¼in) from the edge. Sew a second row 3mm (⅛in) below the first. Hold the threads tightly on the top of the fabric and gently gather the material until it is the same width as the bottom of the yoke piece, with the gathers evenly distributed.

Cut two pieces of bias binding to fit the bottom of the yokes. With right sides together, align the bottom of the yoke to the top of the front bodice pieces, with the raw edges of the bias binding wedged between; sew along the seam allowance (see figure 1).

Repeat for the lining, excluding the bias-binding trim.

STEP 2
Constructing the bodice

With right sides together, align the notches at the shoulders and sew the top edge of the front yoke to the top of the back bodice with a 5mm (¼in) seam allowance (see *figure 2*).

Sew the side seams of the bodice together with a 5mm (¼in) seam allowance.

Repeat for the lining. Press all the seams open on the outer piece and the lining.

With wrong sides together, put the lining into the bodice and baste all the way around.

figure 2

figure 3

STEP 3
Adding the sleeves

In the same way as you gathered the front bodice (see *step 1*), loosely gather the cap and bottom of each sleeve.

Cut a length of bias binding to fit around the bottom edge of the sleeve. Fold and press one side of the trim 5mm (¼in) into the centre fold. Align the raw edge of the trim on the right side with the inside of the bottom edge of the sleeve, and sew it in place, stitching 5mm (¼in) from the edge. Flip the folded side of the trim to the outside and topstitch around the sleeve.

With wrong sides together, sew the front and back of the sleeves together with a 5mm (¼in) seam allowance. Turn the sleeve inside out so right sides are together, and then machine stitch 5mm (¼in) from the seam to enclose the raw edges.

With right sides together, fit the sleeves into the armholes and sew with an 8mm (⅛in) seam allowance (see *figure 3*). Press the seams away from the bodice and overlock the raw edges.

STEP 4

Making the button plackets

Fold and press the centre edge of the front bodices 5mm (¼in) to the wrong side, and then press the button plackets to the wrong side along the fold lines. Topstitch along the folded edges (see *figure 4*).

Make four vertical buttonholes in the right button placket, positioning the first centrally 5mm (¼in) from the top and spacing the others evenly 5cm (2in) apart. Sew four corresponding buttons onto the left placket.

figure 4

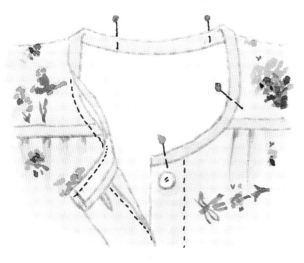

figure 5

STEP 5

Finishing the neckline

Cut a length of bias binding long enough to go all the way around the neckline with an additional 5mm (¼in) at each end. Fold and press each end 5mm (¼in) to the wrong side. Fold and press one side of the trim 5mm (¼in) into the centre fold. Align the raw edge of the trim on the right side with the inside of the neckline; sew in place, stitching 5mm (¼in) from the edge. Flip the folded side of the trim to the outside and topstitch around the neckline (see *figure 5*).

STEP 6

Finishing the shirt

Fold and press the bottom edge of the shirt 5mm (¼in) to the wrong side. Fold over and press another 2cm (¾in) and machine stitch all the way around the hem.

Cut a length of bias binding to fit around the edge of the pocket. Encase the edge of the pocket within the centre fold of the bias binding; pin and then baste in place, tucking the raw edges to the wrong side at the point at the bottom of the pocket. Machine stitch the trim in place along the top curve of the pocket.

Position the pocket on the right-hand front bodice, with the point approximately 5cm (2in) from the bottom, and pin in place (see *figure 6*). Topstitch the pocket onto the bodice around the sides and bottom, starting and finishing where the machine stitching begins and ends.

figure 6

STEP 7

Sewing up the pyjama bottoms

With right sides together, sew the front and back of the pyjama bottoms together along the side seams with a 5mm (¼in) seam allowance.

Starting at the waistline and with right sides together, sew the left and right of the pyjama bottoms together along the centre front and centre back seams with a 5mm (¼in) seam allowance.

With right sides together, starting at the bottom of the right leg, pin and then baste the front right leg to the back right leg up to the crotch. Match up the centre front and centre back seams, and continue from the crotch down the left leg to the ankle, attaching the left front to the left back (see figure 7). Machine stitch with a 5mm (¼in) seam allowance.

At the waistline, fold the material 5mm (¼in) to the wrong side and press. Press all the seams open. Repeat for the lining.

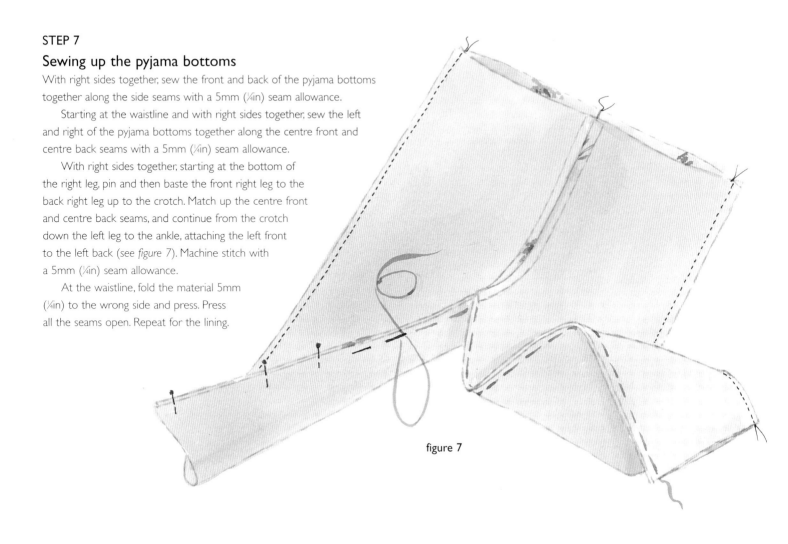

figure 7

figure 8

STEP 8

Making the waistband

With wrong sides together, put the pyjama bottoms into the lining and pin and then baste together at the waistline. Machine stitch along the 5mm (¼in) fold to hem the waistline.

Fold the edge over again, far enough to accommodate the width of the elastic. Machine stitch along the folded edge of the waistband, leaving 2.5cm (1in) open at the centre back.

Using a safety pin, thread the elastic through the channel (see figure 8) and sew the ends over one another at the centre back. Machine stitch the centre back closed.

figure 9

STEP 9

Finishing the pyjama bottoms

Cut two pieces of 5mm- (¼in-) wide elastic a few centimetres smaller than the width of the bottom of the pyjama legs. Pin one piece around the inside of each pyjama leg, 2cm (¾in) from the bottom edge. Stretching the elastic tight as you sew, secure with two parallel rows of machine stitching, overlapping the ends of the elastic at the side seam (see figure 9).

Apply a serge stitch or decorative stay stitch to the hems to cover the raw edges of the material and lining.

Sleep Tight Bedtime Drink

There's nothing like a comforting warm drink to ensure a good night's sleep. If bedtime becomes a battle ground, this can be part of your nightly routine, along with a favourite story — your child will be drifting off to dreamland in no time at all.

Heat a small mug's worth of milk (choose soy or rice milk if your child is lactose intolerant) over a low to medium heat in a non-stick saucepan, until it is just bubbling at the edges. Either serve the milk neat, or sweeten to taste with a little organic honey or a couple of squares of dark chocolate melted into it for a special treat. Chop or grate the chocolate and place it in the mug; pour the warm milk over it and stir well.

Wee Willie Winkie runs through the town,
Upstairs and downstairs in his nightgown,
Tapping at the window and crying through the lock,
Are all the children in their beds, it's past eight o'clock?

Laundry/Toy Bag

Roomy catch-all bags such as this are invaluable in a child's room and are especially useful for collecting dirty laundry or storing toys. You can let your imagination run wild when selecting a fabric for this project – a vintage-style print will add to the décor of the room and can be chosen to match or enhance a handmade duvet cover and pillowcase set (see page 116).

Customizing the bag with the child's initials is practical in a large family, especially when a bedroom or playroom is shared, and also transforms it into a personalized gift.

Materials

Printed cotton poplin
Contrasting cotton fabric for
    appliqué initials (approximately
    15 x 15cm/6 x 6in for each initial)
Iron-on fabric adhesive (15 x
    15cm/6 x 6in for each initial)
Card for appliqué templates (15 x
    15cm/6 x 6in for each initial)
Pen, craft knife and cutting mat
Fabric marker pen
Basting thread
Matching sewing thread
Contrasting thread for appliqué
Sewing machine and sewing kit
Iron and ironing board
Safety pin

figure 1

STEP 1
Applying the appliqué decoration

Apply iron-on fabric adhesive to the back of your appliqué fabric, following the manufacturer's instructions.

Either hand-draw or trace your child's initials onto a piece of card and cut it out to make templates. Place the templates wrong side up on the adhesive side of your fabric (so that the letter will be the right way round on the right side of the fabric). Draw around the outline of the templates with a fabric marker pen and cut out the shapes (see *figure 1*).

Pin and tack the initials right side up onto the centre of the front piece of the bag. Following the manufacturer's instructions, apply the iron to fuse the initials in place, and then remove the tacking.

Choose a contrasting thread and set the sewing machine to a small to medium zigzag stitch that is close together; machine stitch around the edge of each initial, covering the raw edges.

STEP 2

Constructing the bag

Cut two rectangles of fabric measuring 74 × 64cm (29¼ × 25½in). With right sides together, sew the sides and bottom of the bag together with a 1cm (½in) seam allowance, but leave 1cm (½in) at the end of one side seam unstitched. Repeat for the lining. Press all the seams open. Topstitch along the seam allowance on both pieces where the side seam has not been sewn to keep the raw edges neatly on the inside.

Place the lining into the bag with wrong sides together; match up the side seams and pin and then baste around the top edge (see *figure 2*).

figure 2

figure 3

STEP 3

Making the drawstring channel

Cut out a strip of fabric 128 × 8cm (50½ × 3in) on the cross grain. Fold and press the ends 2cm (¾in) to the wrong side. Fold and press the strip in half lengthways. Open it out and press one side 5mm (¼in) into the centre fold.

Hold the strip so the raw edge is at the top and the right side of the strip is facing the right side of the lining. Line up the ends of the band with the little opening in the side seams and sew the band around the inside of the bag, stitching 5mm (¼in) from the edge.

Flip the folded edge of the band over to the right side of the bag and pin (see *figure 3*); topstitch along the folded edge and 5mm (¼in) above it.

STEP 4

Making the drawstring

Cut a strip of fabric 154 × 3cm (62 × 1¼in) on the cross grain. Fold and press both ends of the strip 5mm (¼in) to the wrong side. Fold and press the strip in half lengthways, with wrong sides together. Open it out and fold both raw edges into the centre fold, and then press it in half again so the width is in quarters (see *figure 4*). Topstitch along the length and ends of the strip.

Use a safety pin to thread the drawstring through the channel.

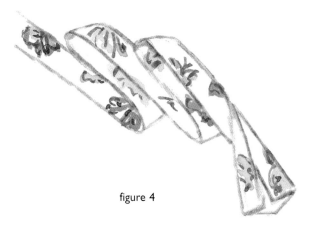

figure 4

ship ahoy!

treasure chest

Tooth Fairy Pillow

What could be more magical when there is a wobbly tooth in the house than for the tooth-wobbler to have this wonderful, personal little pillow in which to place their precious item when the time comes for a visit from the tooth fairy? It means the tooth won't get lost overnight and the 'fairy' will be able to find it easily while your child is sleeping, leaving a small monetary reward in the pocket as a surprise in the morning. It's such a lovely keepsake for Mum, too, so make it in your child's favourite fabric to make it even more special.

Materials

2 squares of fabric for the cushion
    front and back, 21 x 21cm
    (8¼ x 8¼in)
1 piece of fabric for the pocket,
    10 x 8cm (4 x 3in)
Wadding or dried lavender
    for the filling
85cm (33½in) ribbon or trim,
    2.5cm (1in) wide
1 button, 5cm (2in) diameter
Small length of contrasting ribbon
    (to tie around centre of button)
Matching machine thread
Contrasting thread for decorative
    stitching
Sewing machine and sewing kit
Iron and ironing board

figure 1

STEP 1

Making the pocket

Fold and press all four sides of the pocket 5mm (¼in) to the wrong side. Then fold over and press the top of the pocket an additional 1cm (½in) and machine stitch.

Pin the pocket onto the centre of the front piece of the pillow, right sides up (see figure 1). Topstitch along the sides and bottom of the pocket.

Using contrasting thread, machine stitch a wavy line of stitching around the sides and bottom of the pocket.

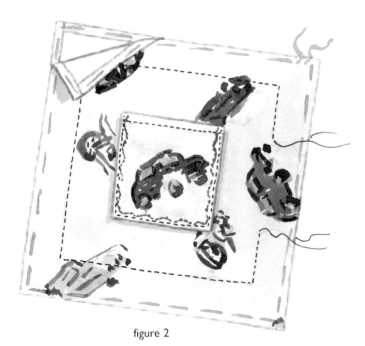

figure 2

STEP 2

Sewing the pillow together

Fold and press all four sides of the front and back of the pillow 5mm (¼in) to the wrong side and baste.

Place the front of the pillow on top of the back, with wrong sides together, making sure the edges are perfectly aligned, and pin together. Leaving a 5cm (2in) gap in one side, machine stitch all the way around with a 2cm (¾in) seam allowance (see *figure 2*).

Either stuff the pillow with wadding or, using a funnel, fill it with dried lavender, then machine stitch the gap closed.

STEP 3

Trimming the pillow

Cut a length of 2.5cm- (1in-) wide ribbon long enough to go all the way around the edge of the pillow, allowing sufficient to mitre the corners. Pin the ribbon or trim in place on the front of the pillow, folding it back on itself diagonally at the corners and folding the end under diagonally to match (see *figure 3*).

Topstitch all the way around the outer edge of the ribbon, sewing through all three layers. Topstitch along the diagonal folds at each corner.

figure 3

figure 4

STEP 4

Decorating the pillow

Thread the sewing machine with contrasting thread, and sew two parallel wavy lines 5mm (¼in) in from both edges of the ribbon (see *figure 4*).

Tack bows or sew buttons on as desired. We used a large yellow button in the top right corner. For extra colour, we tied the centre of the oversized button with red ribbon and hand-stitched that to the pillow.

Templates

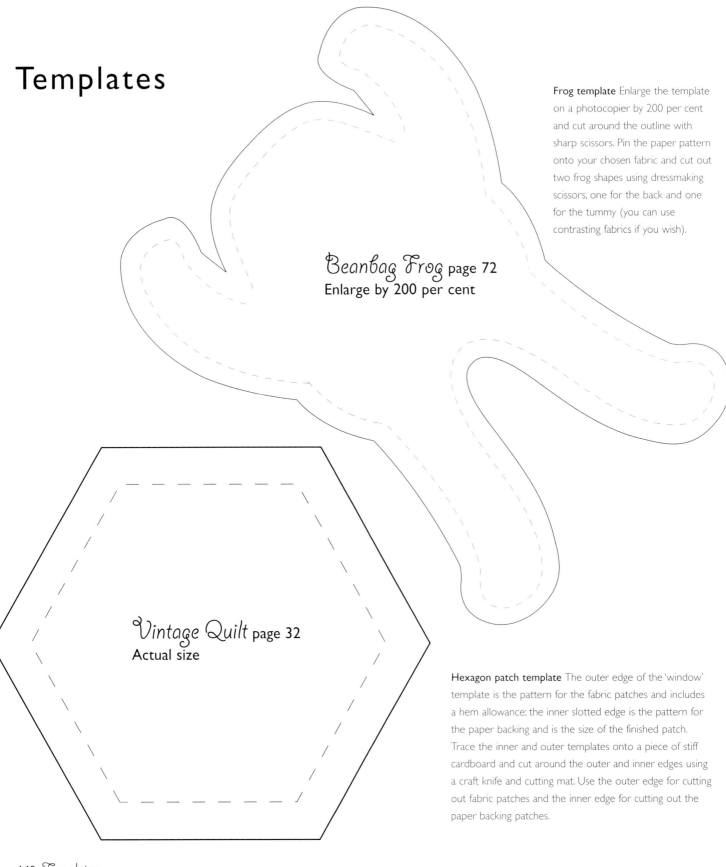

Frog template Enlarge the template on a photocopier by 200 per cent and cut around the outline with sharp scissors. Pin the paper pattern onto your chosen fabric and cut out two frog shapes using dressmaking scissors, one for the back and one for the tummy (you can use contrasting fabrics if you wish).

Beanbag Frog page 72
Enlarge by 200 per cent

Vintage Quilt page 32
Actual size

Hexagon patch template The outer edge of the 'window' template is the pattern for the fabric patches and includes a hem allowance; the inner slotted edge is the pattern for the paper backing and is the size of the finished patch. Trace the inner and outer templates onto a piece of stiff cardboard and cut around the outer and inner edges using a craft knife and cutting mat. Use the outer edge for cutting out fabric patches and the inner edge for cutting out the paper backing patches.

Sewing Guidelines & Tips

If you need to brush up your sewing skills, begin with some of the easier projects such as the Notice Board (page 70), Beanbag Frog (page 72), Duvet Set (page 116) and Laundry/Toy Bag (page 132). The following tips will help to clarify any terms or stitches that may be unfamiliar.

- Unless otherwise stated, when the instruction is to 'sew', it is recommended to pin, baste and then machine stitch with a straight medium-length running stitch. When the machine stitching is complete, remove the basting thread using an unpicker.

- Raw edges of seams can be finished in one of two ways: either press the seam to one side (usually to the back of the garment) and use an overlocking stitch on your sewing machine, stitching both sides of the seam together; or press the seam open and set your sewing machine to a medium-length zigzag stitch and sew along both raw edges.

- Overlock or serge stitching is used to finish a raw edge and requires a special type of sewing machine (called a serger). You can substitute this stitch with zigzag stitching.

- Basting can be done by hand or on the sewing machine. Use a contrasting thread that is easy to break and sew long, straight stitches. Basting holds the seam together temporarily before machine stitching and is easier to sew over than pins. Remove the basting thread after machine stitching using an unpicker.

- Tacking (another term for basting) is used to hold pieces together temporarily before machine stitching. In this book, the term tacking is used when two or more pieces – for example, a button placket – need to be held in place with a couple of hand-stitches before sewing.

- Gathering stitching is used to create an even fullness on skirts and to fit sleeves into armholes and bodice pieces into yokes, for example. As with basting, you can sew gathering stitching by hand or on the sewing machine using a long stitch length. Leave long threads at both ends of each row of stitching and sew one row 5mm (¼in) in from the raw edge that is to be gathered. Sew a second row 3mm (⅛in) below the first. Hold both threads at one end of the rows on the same side of the fabric, and pull them gently to gather up the fabric to the required width. When you come to stitch the seam, sew with an 8mm (⅜in) seam allowance, stitching over the second row of gathering stitches. If you use matching thread, you don't need to unpick the gathering stitching after sewing the seams.

- The bottom of skirts, trousers, sleeves, and so on are usually hemmed. Unless otherwise stated, fold and press the raw edge 5mm (¼in) to the wrong side. Then fold over and press another 5mm (¼in) and

machine stitch along the edge. If you find it easier, you can fold and press the edge 1cm (½in) to the wrong side, then fold the raw edge into the crease line, press and then machine stitch in place.

- All neck and sleeve bindings need to be cut on the bias so that they can be eased around curves. This means that the paper pattern piece must be positioned diagonally across the weave of the fabric.

- Blanket stitch can be used to decorate the edges of collars, pockets or hems (see step 8 on page 86). It can also be used for appliqué. Mark a stitch guideline parallel to the edge of the fabric. Use two strands of embroidery thread and anchor the knot on the underside close to the edge to be stitched. Working from left to right, bring the needle out to the front of the fabric very close to the edge. Put the needle back in on the upper line, one space to the right, and bring it through to the front again with the tip of the needle over the top of the working thread. Space the stitches evenly along the row and then fasten the thread securely on the underside.

- Stay stitching is a single line of stitching along the edge of a piece of fabric that has been cut on the bias – around a neckline, for example. The stitching helps to stabilize the fabric and prevents it from distorting. It ensures that necklines keep their shapes and that pieces such as collars and facings fit together correctly.

Equipment

Sewing machine – Use a sewing machine with straight and zigzag stitches, plus an ordinary presser foot, zipper foot and embroidery foot. Choose a long stitch length to sew gathering stitching and a medium-length stitch for seams and topstitching. Always use a sharp, new needle when sewing delicate fabrics such as organza, silk or satin, so as not to damage the fabric. Serger sewing machines are capable of serge stitching, which is a way of finishing raw edges by overlocking; you can substitute this on a regular sewing machine by using zigzag stitching.

Threads – Unless contrasting thread is called for (for appliqué or decorative stitching, for example) match your thread carefully to your chosen fabric, so that your stitches are as invisible as possible on the finished garment; good-quality polyester thread is fine. For basting, use a contrasting colour of thread that is easy to break, so it can be removed easily after machine stitching.

Iron and ironing board – An iron is essential for pressing seams after stitching and for applying iron-on interfacing or iron-on adhesive for appliqué. Make sure the iron is set to the correct temperature for your chosen fabric. Always iron velvet on the reverse.

Sewing Kit

Dressmaker's scissors – A large sharp pair for cutting out fabric.

Fabric marker pen – To temporarily mark fabric and to draw around templates; these fade or wipe off with a damp cloth.

Needles – For hand-sewing, basting and sewing on buttons. Use fine needles for delicate fabrics and stronger ones for thicker materials.

Pins – For pinning seams and trims in place before sewing. Remove pins just before machine-stitching delicate fabrics, so that they don't get caught and tear the fabric.

Safety pins – For threading elastic or drawstrings through casings.

Small scissors – A sharp pair for cutting thread and trimmings.

Tape measure – Use a flexible tape measure for taking your child's measurements, for measuring the distance between pin-tucks, and for measuring lengths of lace or trim.

Thimble – For pushing the end of a needle through tough fabric or layers of material.

Unpicker or seam ripper – Useful for unpicking stitches, breaking basting thread and making buttonholes.

Making the Paper Patterns

Patterns for 19 of the garments can be found on the enclosed disc in PDF format. PDF patterns are viewable using Adobe Reader, which can be downloaded free of charge from http://get.adobe.com/reader/. The patterns can be printed on A4 or Letter paper on your home printer and pieced together.

Babies' clothes are given in sizes 0–3 months, 3–6 months, 6–9 months, 9–12 months and 12–18 months. Girls' and boys' clothes are given in sizes 18–24 months, 3–4 years, 5–6 years and 7–8 years. See the size guide below.

Open your chosen pattern in the correct size and print off all the pages. Referring to the scaled-down diagram, tape the pages together to make up the pattern pieces by matching up the numbers in the corners of each page and aligning the corresponding sections of the pattern. Spread out all the pages on the floor first in the correct order, before trimming the sections and taping them together. Cut out the paper pattern pieces and pin them onto your fabric as indicated. The arrow on each pattern piece indicates the direction of the grain of the fabric: position the paper pattern on the fabric accordingly.

Size Guide

Height: Measure from the top of the child's head to the ground, but ensure they are not wearing shoes.

Chest: Measure the widest part of the chest.

Waist: Measure just above the hip bone, which is the natural waistline.

Age	Height	Chest	Waist
0–3 months	62cm/24½in	–	–
3–6 months	68cm/26¾in	–	–
6–9 months	74cm/29¼in	–	–
9–12 months	80cm/31½in	–	–
12–18 months	86cm/34in	50cm/19¾in	46cm/18¼in
18–24 months	92cm/36¼in	52cm/20½in	48cm/19in
3–4 years	104cm/41in	55cm/21¾in	52cm/20½in
5–6 years	116cm/45½in	60cm/23¾in	56cm/22in
7–8 years	128cm/50½in	64cm/25¼in	58cm/22¾in

Address Book

Their Nibs
214 Kensington Park Road
London
W11 1NR
020 7221 4263

79 Chamberlayne Road
London
NW10 3ND
020 8964 8444
www.theirnibs.com
Fabric and clothes available online.

Fabrics & Haberdashery

The Button Queen
76 Marylebone Lane
London
W1U 2PR
020 7935 1505
www.thebuttonqueen.co.uk
Vintage and modern buttons.

The Cloth House
47 Berwick Street
London
W1F 8SJ
020 7437 5155
www.clothhouse.com
Fabrics and vintage trims.

Hobbycraft
01202 596100
Online orders: 0845 051 6599
www.hobbycraft.co.uk
Arts and crafts superstore
with online store and
branches nationwide.

John Lewis
Oxford Street
London
W1A 1EX
(and Branches Nationwide)
020 7629 7711
www.johnlewis.com
Main stockists of Their Nibs
fabrics and a great general
haberdashery department.

Liberty
Regent Street
London
W1B 5AH
020 7734 1234
www.liberty.co.uk
Haberdashery and fabrics, including
the famous Liberty prints.

Temptation Alley
361 Portobello Road
London
W10 5SA
020 8964 2004
A treasure-trove of haberdashery.

VV Rouleaux
54 Sloane Square
Cliveden Place
London
SW1W 8AX
020 7730 3125
www.vvrouleaux.com
Ribbons and trims specialist.

Vintage Furniture & Other Items

Circus Antiques
60 Chamberlayne Road
London
NW10 3JH
0208 968 8244
www.circusantiques.co.uk
Furniture and interior objects
from the nineteenth and
twentieth century.

Howie and Belle
52 Chamberlayne Road
London
NW10 3JH
020 8964 4553
www.howieandbelle.com
Antique objects and furniture,
as well as vintage clothing
and accessories.

Niche Antiques
70 Chamberlayne Road
London
NW10 3JJ
020 3181 0081
www.nicheantiques.co.uk
Vintage furniture and
home accessories.

Shona Patterson
shonapatterson@btconnect.com
020 8960 2100
Shona sources vintage clothes
and accessories for kids and is
a constant source of inspiration.

Sunbury Antiques Market
Kempton Park Racecourse
Staines Road
East Sunbury on Thames
Middlesex
TW16 5AQ
01932 230946
www.kemptonantiques.com
For fabulous vintage finds
from France and the UK.

Other Places to Look for Inspiration

Chiswick Car Boot Sale
Chiswick Community School
Burlington Lane
London
W4 3UN

eBay.co.uk

Portobello Road Market
Portobello Road/Westbourne Grove
London W11
020 7229 8354
www.portobelloroad.co.uk

Vintage fairs
Look out for vintage fairs in
Clerkenwell, Hammersmith, Kings
Road in Chelsea, and local to you.

Acknowledgements

Thank you to:

Jacqui – for seeing the opportunity for this book;

Vanessa – for your incredible shots and bringing the clothes to life;

Barbara – for your amazing innovative design;

Zia – for your patience and understanding;

Kerenza – for your calmness;

Sara – for your fantastic organizing skills.

To my husband Charlie and son Finn, for their amazing and continued inspiration and love.

To my Dad, who helped me start Their Nibs and continues to be a great help to the business; and my Mum, who gave me my love of eclectic clothes and prints – in addition to their love and support over the years.

To our gorgeous models:

Isadora Bartleet

Tabitha Bell

Gabriel Bennett

Noah Bennett

Joni Bingle

Bluebell Carrol

Cassidy Carrol

Katie Czajkowska

Mekhi Forde

Isabella Heath

Harland Hichens

Katherine Hichens

Esme Potter

Katie Salamon Andrew

Jude Slade

Jasmin Tarabanov

Sol Tarabanov

Isabela Whately

Thanks also to:

Camilla Daniel at Bruce and Brown Models;

Mark Slade at Circus Antiques and Polly at Niche Antiques;

Elizabeth Ward, our American intern who made the beautiful quilt;

Shona Patterson, vintage kids' clothing specialist and Their Nibs agent;

Selene Allen, Aislyn Gibson and Debi Treloar, for the use of your beautiful homes for our locations;

Clare O'Connell, for your cakes at: http://little-bakers.blogspot.com/.